How to access your on-line resources

Kaplan Financial students will have a MyKaplan account and these extra resources will be available to you online. You do not need to register again, as this process was completed when you enrolled. If you are having problems accessing online materials, please ask your course administrator.

If you are not studying with Kaplan and did not purchase your book via a Kaplan website, to unlock your extra online resources please go to www.en-gage.co.uk (even if you have set up an account and registered books previously). You will then need to enter the ISBN number (on the title page and back cover) and the unique pass key number contained in the scratch panel below to gain access.

You will also be required to enter additional information during this process to set up or confirm your account details.

If you purchased through the Kaplan Publishing website you will automatically receive an e-mail invitation to register your details and gain access to your content. If you do not receive the e-mail or book content, please contact Kaplan Publishing.

Your code and information

This code can only be used once for the registration of one book online. This registration and your online content will expire when the final sittings for the examinations covered by this book have taken place. Please allow one hour from the time you submit your book details for us to process your request.

Please scratch the film to access your unique code.

Please be aware that this code is case-sensitive and you will need to include the dashes within the passcode, but not when entering the ISBN.

KAPLAN

PUBLISHING

Strategic Level

Subject F3

Financial Strategy

EXAM PRACTICE KIT

CIMA
PUBLISHING

KAPLAN
PUBLISHING

British Library Cataloguing-in-Publication Data

A catalogue record for this book is available from the British Library.

Published by:

Kaplan Publishing UK
Unit 2 The Business Centre
Molly Millar's Lane
Wokingham
Berkshire
RG41 2QZ

ISBN: 978-1-78740-728-2

Kaplan Publishing's learning materials are designed to help students succeed in their examinations. In certain circumstances, CIMA can make post-exam adjustment to a student's mark or grade to reflect adverse circumstances which may have disadvantaged a student's ability to take an exam or demonstrate their normal level of attainment (see CIMA's Special Consideration policy). However, it should be noted that students will not be eligible for special consideration by CIMA if preparation for or performance in a CIMA exam is affected by any failure by their tuition provider to prepare them properly for the exam for any reason including, but not limited to, staff shortages, building work or a lack of facilities etc.

Similarly, CIMA will not accept applications for special consideration on any of the following grounds:

- failure by a tuition provider to cover the whole syllabus

- failure by the student to cover the whole syllabus, for instance as a result of joining a course part way through

- failure by the student to prepare adequately for the exam, or to use the correct pre-seen material

- errors in the Kaplan Official Study Text, including sample (practice) questions or any other Kaplan content or

- errors in any other study materials (from any other tuition provider or publisher).

CONTENTS

	Page

Section

Quality and accuracy are of the utmost importance to us so if you spot an error in any of our products, please send an email to mykaplanreporting@kaplan.com with full details.

Our Quality Co-ordinator will work with our technical team to verify the error and take action to ensure it is corrected in future editions.

INDEX TO QUESTIONS AND ANSWERS

OBJECTIVE TEST QUESTIONS

EXAM TECHNIQUES

COMPUTER-BASED ASSESSMENT

Golden rules

1 Make sure you have completed the compulsory 15-minute tutorial before you start the test. This tutorial is available through the CIMA website and focusses on the functionality of the exam. You cannot speak to the invigilator once you have started.

2 These exam practice kits give you plenty of exam style questions to practise so make sure you use them to fully prepare.

3 Attempt all questions, there is no negative marking.

4 Double check your answer before you put in the final answer although you can change your response as many times as you like.

5 Not all questions will be multiple choice questions (MCQs) – you may have to fill in missing words or figures.

6 Identify the easy questions first and get some points on the board to build up your confidence.

7 Attempt 'wordy' questions first as these may be quicker than the computation style questions. This will relieve some of the time pressure you will be under during the exam.

8 If you don't know the answer, flag the question and attempt it later. In your final review before the end of the exam try a process of elimination.

9 Work out your answer on the whiteboard provided first if it is easier for you. There is also an onscreen 'scratch pad' on which you can make notes. You are not allowed to take pens, pencils, rulers, pencil cases, phones, paper or notes into the testing room.

SYLLABUS GUIDANCE, LEARNING OBJECTIVES AND VERBS

A   CIMA 2019 PROFESSIONAL QUALIFICATION

Details regarding the content of the CIMA 2019 professional qualification can be located within the CIMA 2019 professional qualification syllabus document.

You can use the following diagram showing the whole structure of your qualification to help you keep track of your progress. Make sure you seek appropriate advice if you are unsure about your progression through the qualification.

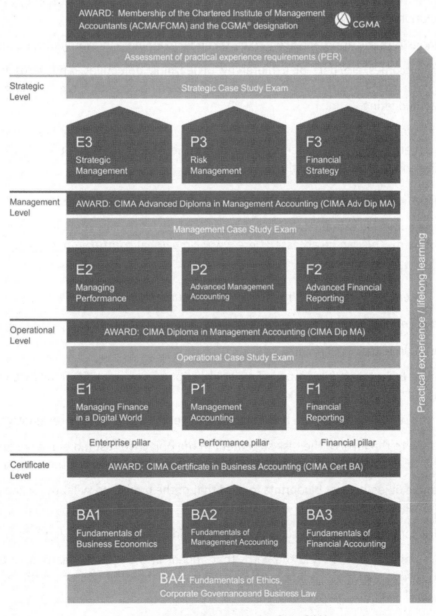

Reproduced with permission from CIMA

B   STUDY WEIGHTINGS

A percentage weighting is shown against each exam content area in the exam blueprint. This is intended as a guide to the proportion of study time each topic requires.

All component learning outcomes will be tested.

The weightings do not specify the number of marks that will be allocated to topics in the examination.

C   LEARNING OUTCOMES

Each subject within the qualification is divided into a number of broad syllabus topics. The topics contain one or more lead learning outcomes, related component learning outcomes and indicative knowledge content.

A learning outcome has two main purposes:

1   to define the skill or ability that a well-prepared candidate should be able to exhibit in the examination

2   to demonstrate the approach likely to be taken by examiners in examination questions.

The learning outcomes are part of a hierarchy of learning objectives. The verbs used at the beginning of each learning outcome relate to a specific learning objective, e.g. Evaluate alternative approaches to budgeting.

The verb 'evaluate' indicates a high-level learning objective. As learning objectives are hierarchical, it is expected that at this level students will have knowledge of different budgeting systems and methodologies and be able to apply them.

The examination blueprints and representative task statements

CIMA have also published examination blueprints giving learners clear expectations regarding what is expected of them. This can be accessed here www.cimaglobal.com/examblueprints

The blueprint is structured as follows:

*   Exam content sections (reflecting the syllabus document)

*   Lead and component outcomes (reflecting the syllabus document)

*   Representative task statements.

A representative task statement is a plain English description of what a CIMA finance professional should know and be able to do.

The content and skill level determine the language and verbs used in the representative task.

CIMA will test up to the level of the task statement in the objective test (an objective test question on a particular topic could be set at a lower level than the task statement in the blueprint).

The format of the objective test blueprints follows that of the published syllabus for the 2019 CIMA Professional Qualification.

Weightings for content sections are also included in the individual subject blueprints.

A list of the learning objectives and the verbs that appear in the syllabus learning outcomes and examinations follows and these will help you to understand the depth and breadth required for a topic and the skill level the topic relates to.

CIMA verb hierarchy

Skill level	Verbs used	Definition
Level 5 Evaluation How you are expected to use your learning to evaluate, make decisions or recommendations	Advise	Counsel, inform or notify
	Assess	Evaluate or estimate the nature, ability or quality of
	Evaluate	Appraise or assess the value of
	Recommend	Propose a course of action
	Review	Assess and evaluate in order, to change if necessary
Level 4 Analysis How you are expected to analyse the detail of what you have learned	Align	Arrange in an orderly way
	Analyse	Examine in detail the structure of
	Communicate	Share or exchange information
	Compare and contrast	Show the similarities and/or differences between
	Develop	Grow and expand a concept
	Discuss	Examine in detail by argument
	Examine	Inspect thoroughly
	Interpret	Translate into intelligible or familiar terms
	Monitor	Observe and check the progress of
	Prioritise	Place in order of priority or sequence for action
	Produce	Create or bring into existence
Level 3 Application How you are expected to apply your knowledge	Apply	Put to practical use
	Calculate	Ascertain or reckon mathematically
	Conduct	Organise and carry out
	Demonstrate	Prove with certainty or exhibit by practical means
	Prepare	Make or get ready for use
	Reconcile	Make or prove consistent/compatible
Level 2 Comprehension What you are expected to understand	Describe	Communicate the key features of
	Distinguish	Highlight the differences between
	Explain	Make clear or intelligible/state the meaning or purpose of
	Identify	Recognise, establish or select after consideration
	Illustrate	Use an example to describe or explain something
Level 1 Knowledge What you are expected to know	List	Make a list of
	State	Express, fully or clearly, the details/facts of
	Define	Give the exact meaning of
	Outline	Give a summary of

D OBJECTIVE TEST

Objective test

Objective test questions require you to choose or provide a response to a question whose correct answer is predetermined.

The most common types of objective test question you will see are:

- Multiple choice, where you have to choose the correct answer(s) from a list of possible answers. This could either be numbers or text.

- Multiple response, for example, choosing two correct answers from a list of eight possible answers. This could either be numbers or text.

- Fill in the blank, where you fill in your answer within the provided space.

- Drag and drop, for example, matching a technical term with the correct definition.

- Hot spots, where you select an answer by clicking on graphs/diagrams.

Guidance re CIMA on-screen calculator

As part of the CIMA objective test software, candidates are now provided with a calculator. This calculator is on-screen and is available for the duration of the assessment. The calculator is available in each of the objective tests and is accessed by clicking the calculator button in the top left hand corner of the screen at any time during the assessment. Candidates are permitted to utilise personal calculators as long as they are an approved CIMA model. CIMA approved model list is found here: https://www.cimaglobal.com/Studying/study-and-resources/.

All candidates must complete a 15-minute exam tutorial before the assessment begins and will have the opportunity to familiarise themselves with the calculator and practise using it. The exam tutorial is also available online via the CIMA website. Candidates can use their own calculators providing it is included in CIMA's authorised calculator listing.

Fundamentals of objective tests

The objective tests are 90-minute assessments comprising 60 compulsory questions, with one or more parts. There will be no choice and all questions should be attempted. All elements of a question must be answered correctly for the question to be marked correctly. All questions are equally weighted.

APPROACH TO REVISION

Stage 1: Assess areas of strengths and weaknesses

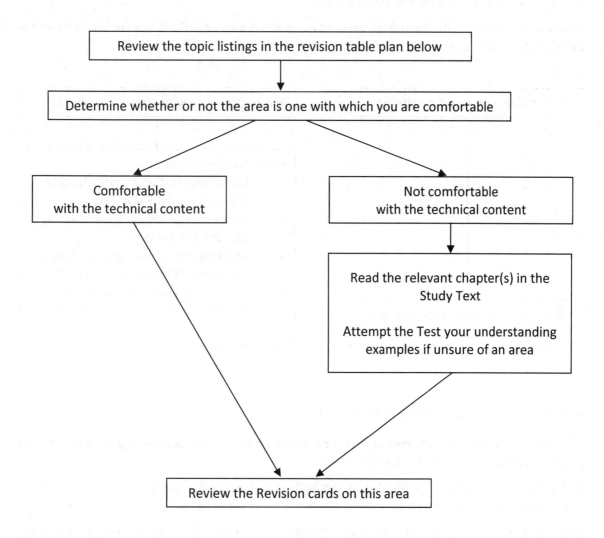

Review the topic listings in the revision table plan below

Determine whether or not the area is one with which you are comfortable

Comfortable
with the technical content

Not comfortable
with the technical content

Read the relevant chapter(s) in the
Study Text

Attempt the Test your understanding
examples if unsure of an area

Review the Revision cards on this area

Stage 2: Question practice

Follow the order of revision of topics as recommended in the revision table plan below and attempt the questions in the order suggested.

Try to avoid referring to text books and notes and the model answer until you have completed your attempt.

Try to answer the question in the allotted time.

Review your attempt with the model answer and assess how much of the answer you achieved in the allocated exam time.

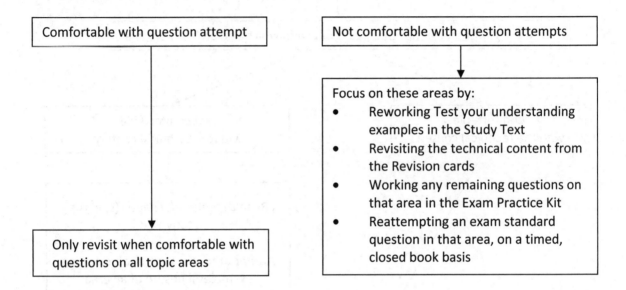

Stage 3: Final pre-exam revision

We recommend that you **attempt at least one ninety minute mock examination** containing a set of previously unseen exam standard questions.

It is important that you get a feel for the breadth of coverage of a real exam without advanced knowledge of the topic areas covered – just as you will expect to see on the real exam day.

Ideally a mock examination offered by your tuition provider should be sat in timed, closed book, real exam conditions.

Information concerning formulae and tables will be provided via the CIMA website:
www.cimaglobal.com.

SYLLABUS GRIDS

F3: Financial Strategy

Create financial strategy, evaluate and manage financial risk and assess organisational value

Content weighting

Content area		Weighting
A	Financial policy decisions	15%
B	Sources of long-term funds	25%
C	Financial risks	20%
D	Business valuation	40%
		100%

F3A: Financial policy decisions

The overall strategy of the organisation must be supported by how its finances are organised. This requires an understanding of the different strategic financial objectives and policy options that are open to organisations. The choice of these objectives and policy options will be heavily influenced by the financial market requirements and the regulatory environment in which the organisation operates. This section examines these issues.

Lead outcome	Component outcome	Topics to be covered	Explanatory notes
1. Advise on strategic financial objectives.	a. Analyse different types of organisations and their objectives. b. Advise on financial objectives. c. Advise on non-financial objectives.	• Profit and not-for-profit organisations • Quoted and unquoted companies • Private and public sector organisations • Value for money, maximising shareholder wealth • Earnings growth, dividend growth • Impact of underlying economic conditions and business variables on financial objectives • Enhancing the value of other non-financial capitals (human capital, intellectual capital and social and relationship capital) • United Nations Sustainability Development Goals	This section is about aligning financial objectives and policies to the strategies of the organisation. The key aim is to make sure that the organisation has a proper basis to determine what types of funds to access and how to use those funds. To do this effectively finance professionals must be able to evaluate the opportunities and constraints placed on them in the operating environment – particularly financial market requirements, the impact of taxation and the requirements of industry and financial market regulators.
2. Analyse strategic financial policy decisions.	Analyse the following policy decision areas: a. Investment b. Financing c. Dividends d. Interrelationships between policy decision areas	• Use of policy decisions to meet cash needs of entity • Sensitivity of forecast financial statements and future cash position to these policy decisions • Consideration of the interests of stakeholders	
3. Discuss the external influences on financial strategic decisions.	Discuss the influence of the following on financial strategic decisions a. Market requirements b. Taxation c. Regulatory requirements	• Lenders' assessment of creditworthiness • Consideration of domestic and international tax regulations • Consideration of industry regulations such as price and service controls	

F3B: Sources of long-term funds

What types of funds are available to organisations to finance the implementation of their strategies? How much of each type should they go for? And what is the impact on the organisation? Where and how do they get these funds? And how do they provide incentives to providers of such funds so that the funds are available at the right time, in the right quantities and at the right cost? These are some of the questions covered by this section.

Lead outcome	Component outcome	Topics to be covered	Explanatory notes
1. Evaluate the capital structure of a firm.	Evaluate: a. Choice of capital structure b. Changes in capital structure	• Capital structure theories (traditional theory and Miller and Modigliani (MM) theories) • Calculation of cost of equity and weighted cost of capital to reflect changes in capital structure • Impact of choice of capital structure on financial statements • Structuring debt/equity profiles of companies in a group	How should important elements of the financial statement be treated in the books? What principles should underpin these? How do financial reporting standards help to ensure this? Using financial reporting standards terminology this part will be looking at issues of recognition and measurement. The most important issues will be considered here.
2. Analyse long-term debt finance.	Analyse: a. Selecting debt instruments b. Target debt profile c. Issuing debt securities d. Debt covenants e. Tax considerations	• Types of debt instruments and criteria for selecting them • Managing interest, currency and refinancing risks with target debt profile • Private placements and capital market issuance of debt • Features of debt covenants	
3. Evaluate equity finance.	a. Evaluate methods of flotation b. Discuss rights issues	• Methods of flotation and implications for management and shareholders • Rights issues, choice of discount rates and impact on shareholders • Calculation of theoretical ex-rights price (TERP) and yield adjusted TERP	
4. Evaluate dividend policy.	Evaluate policy in the following areas: a. Cash dividends b. Scrip dividends c. Share repurchase programmes	• Features and criteria • Impact on shareholder value and entity value, financial statements and performance	

F3B: Sources of long-term funds

F3C: Financial risks

There is always a risk that the organisation will not be able to attract enough funds to finance its operations and in extreme conditions will fail to survive as a result. This section covers the sources of such risks and how to evaluate and manage such financial risks appropriately.

Lead outcome	Component outcome	Topics to be covered	Explanatory notes
1. Discuss the sources and types of financial risks.	Discuss: a. Sources of financial risk b. Types of financial risk	• Economic risk • Political risk • Currency risk • Interest rate risk	Managing risks related to finances is similar to managing other types of risks in general approach and methodology. However, there are specific differences such as the sources and types of financial risks, how they can be quantified and ways in which they are managed. This section looks at the very specific issues related to managing financial risks within a general risk management framework
2. Evaluate financial risks.	a. Evaluate how financial risks are quantified	• Theory and forecasting of exchange rates (e.g. interest rate parity, purchasing power parity and the Fisher Effect) • Value at risk	
3. Recommend ways of managing financial risks.	a. Recommend ways to manage economic and political risks b. Discuss currency risk instruments c. Discuss interest rate risk instruments	• Responses to economic transaction and translation risks • Operations and features of swaps, forward contracts, money market hedges, futures and options • Techniques for combining options in order to achieve specific risk profile such as caps, collars and floors • Internal hedging techniques	

F3C: Financial risks

F3D: Business valuation

The primary objective of all strategic activity is to create and preserve value for organisations. How does the organisation know whether it has succeeded in this objective? Sometimes, in order to implement strategies, organisations have to acquire other organisations. How does the acquirer determine the value of its acquisition? This section covers how to use techniques in business valuation to answer such questions.

Lead outcome	Component outcome	Topics to be covered	Explanatory notes
1. Discuss the context of valuation.	Discuss: a. Listing of firms b. Mergers and acquisitions (M&A) c. Demergers and divestments	• Reasons for M&A and divestments • Taxation implications • Process and implications of management buy-outs • Acquisition by private equity and venture capitalist	This section looks at the conditions under which organisations need to calculate their own value or the value of other organisations or sub-units thereof. It introduces candidates to valuation techniques. Of particular importance in the digital world is the valuation of intangibles. This links also to how to report intangible value and their drivers in integrated reporting. In addition, how should digital assets be valued? One of the reasons for valuation is when merging or acquiring firms. How should such deals be structured, implemented and closed? For example what should the forms of the consideration be? What are the terms of the acquisition? How does one enable benefit realisation, particularly for synergies once the acquired organisation has been integrated into the acquiring organisation?
2. Evaluate the various valuation methods.	a. Evaluate different valuation methods b. Discuss the strengths and weaknesses of each valuation method	• Asset valuation • Valuation of intangibles • Different methods of equity valuation (share prices, earnings valuation, dividend valuation, discounted cash flow valuation) • Capital Asset Pricing Model (CAPM) • Efficient market hypothesis	
3. Analyse pricing and bid issues.	Analyse: a. Pricing issues b. Bid issues	• Forms of consideration • Terms of acquisition • Target entity debt • Methods of financing cash offer and refinancing target entity debt • Bid negotiation	
4. Discuss post-transaction issues.	Discuss: a. Post-transaction value b. Benefit realisation	• Post-transaction value incorporating effect of intended synergies • M&A integration and synergy benefit realisation • Exit strategies	

Section 1

OBJECTIVE TEST QUESTIONS

SYLLABUS SECTION A: FINANCIAL POLICY DECISIONS

1   TTT is a listed company.

In its recent annual report, TTT has defined its three financial objectives as follows:

- To increase dividends by 10% a year.

- To keep gearing below 40%.

- To expand by internal growth and/or by horizontal integration via acquisition of companies operating in the same industry sector.

Which of the following is NOT a valid criticism of TTT's financial objectives?

A   There should be a specific reference made to maximising shareholder wealth

B   The gearing objective is too vague

C   The expansion objective should contain numbers so that its achievement can be measured

D   The dividend growth objective should be linked to company performance

2   **Which TWO of the following are valid differences between the objectives of for-profit and not-for-profit entities?**

A   For-profit entities primarily aim to maximise shareholder wealth whereas not-for-profit entities don't

B   Not-for-profit entities aim to satisfy a wide range of stakeholders whereas for-profit entities only aim to satisfy shareholders

C   Not-for-profit entities don't have financial objectives but for-profit entities do

D   Not-for-profit entities tend to be most concerned about value for money whereas for-profit entities tend to prioritise shareholder wealth maximisation

3   Grand Co reported a profit before interest and tax of $5 million in its most recent accounts. The company is mainly equity financed, but has a $3 million bank borrowing on which it pays 15% per year in interest. The rate of corporate income tax is 20%.

Assuming that Grand Co has an objective to increase post-tax profit by 10% per year, what should be the company's target profit before interest and tax in the current accounting period?

A $5.455 million

B $5.500 million

C $5.250 million

D $5.005 million

4   Heaton Co is a geared company, with 500,000 $1 shares in issue, and a 7% fixed interest rate bank borrowing of $400,000.

It's most recent accounts show a profit before interest and tax of $75,000. The corporate income tax rate is 20%.

In order to achieve an interest cover ratio of 3 next year, what percentage change in profit before interest and tax is required?

A   12.0% increase

B   10.7% increase

C   10.7% decrease

D   12.0% decrease

5   Sebastian Co has just reported the following statement of profit or loss:

	$ million
Revenue	23.6
Operating costs	(8.6)
Operating profit	15.0
Interest (10% on bank borrowings)	(3.4)
Profit before tax	11.6
Tax (25%)	(2.9)
Earnings	8.7

In the coming year, selling prices are expected to rise by 10% and the tax rate is expected to be 28%.

What will be the percentage movement in earnings, assuming everything else remains the same?

A   23.5% decrease

B   7.0% increase

C   13.9% increase

D   16.1% increase

6 Allen Co is a geared company with 1 million $1 shares in issue. Its debt finance comprises $1.5 million (nominal value) of 8% coupon bonds, trading at $108 per cent.

In the most recent accounting period, Allen Co's earnings were $800,000. The corporate income tax rate is 20%.

What was Allen Co's interest cover according to the most recent accounts?

A   6.7 times

B   9.3 times

C   8.3 times

D   9.0 times

7 Chmura Co has just reported the following statement of profit or loss:

	$ million
Revenue	23.6
Operating costs	(8.6)
Operating profit	15.0
Interest (10% on bank borrowings)	(3.4)
Profit before tax	11.6
Tax (25%)	(2.9)
Earnings	8.7

In the coming year, the interest rate on borrowings is expected to rise to 12% and the tax rate is expected to fall to 21%.

What will be the percentage movement in earnings (to the nearest whole number percentage), assuming everything else remains the same?

A   4% decrease

B   1% decrease

C   1% increase

D   No change

8   Jackson Co's statement of profit or loss this year shows:

	$ million
Sales	50
Cost of sales	23
Gross profit	27
Other operating costs	7
Operating profit	20
Financing costs	10
	10
Tax (30%)	3
Earnings	7

Jackson Co's directors expect that they will increase selling prices by 6% at the start of next year, but that there will be no change in the volume of activity.

Also, the government has just announced that the rate of corporate income tax will be cut to 25% next year.

What are the expected earnings of Jackson Co next year?

Enter your answer in $ million to two decimal places.

                                     (INSERT CORRECT FIGURE IN THE BOX)

9   Paragon Co is expecting to make a profit before interest and tax of $10 million in the current year. The rate of corporate income tax is 20%.

The company has $15 million of long dated bonds in issue, with a coupon rate of 9%.

Next year, the directors plan to issue $6 million more long dated bonds, with a coupon rate of 7%, in order to fund an investment project that is expected to increase profit before interest and tax by 5%.

What is the expected profit after tax next year, assuming that the tax rate stays constant?

Enter your answer in $ million to two decimal places.

                                     (INSERT CORRECT FIGURE IN THE BOX)

10   Belle Co has just reported the following statement of profit or loss:

	GBP million
Revenue	60
Operating costs	(35)
Operating profit	25
Interest	(10)
Profit before tax	15
Tax (20%)	(3)
Earnings	12

Although the company's functional currency is the British pound (GBP), half of the reported revenue was generated in the US (denominated in US dollars, USD). The spot rate of exchange at the year end was 1GBP = 1.50 USD.

Next year, the GBP is expected to strengthen by 10% against the USD.

Assuming that all else remains equal (i.e. sales volume, operating costs, interest rate and tax rate), what will be the earnings next year if the exchange rate does move in this way?

A   GBP 9.3 million

B   GBP 9.8 million

C   GBP 14.4 million

D   GBP 15.0 million

11   **What is the effect on prices of US imports and exports when the US dollar depreciates?**

A   Import prices will increase and export prices will decrease

B   Import prices and export prices will increase

C   Import prices will decrease and export prices will increase

D   Import prices and export prices will decrease

12   Squirm Co generated earnings of $2.2 million in 20X1. It has an objective to achieve a compound annual growth in earnings of 5% per annum.

It has just reported an earnings figure of $2.9 million in 20X6.

What is the company's compound annual growth in earnings?

A   31.8%

B   6.4%

C   5.7%

D   4.7%

13   Julie Co has paid the following dividends in recent years:

	20X4	20X5	20X6	20X7	20X8
Dividend per share	0.20	0.22	0.23	0.25	0.28

What is the company's compound annual growth in dividends since 20X4?

A   7.0%

B   10.0%

C   8.0%

D   8.8%

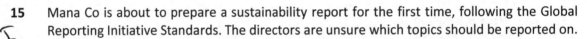

$$4\sqrt{\frac{.28}{.20}} - 1 = 8.8\%$$

14   VUE Co has paid the following dividends in recent years:

	20X4	20X5	20X6	20X7	20X8
Total dividend ($m)	120	130	135	150	170
Number of shares (m)	10	10	10	12	13

What is the company's compound annual growth in dividend per share since 20X4?

A   2.2%

B   6.8%

C   9.0%

D   9.1%

15   Mana Co is about to prepare a sustainability report for the first time, following the Global Reporting Initiative Standards. The directors are unsure which topics should be reported on.

Which of the following Standards will give guidance on which topics are material and should be report on?

A   GRI 101 – Foundation

B   GRI 102 – General Disclosures

C   GRI 103 – Management Approach

D   GRI 200, 300, 400 Series – Topic Specific Standards

16   **Which THREE of the following are objectives of Integrated Reporting, as identified by the International Integrated Reporting Council (IIRC)?**

A   To improve the quality of information available to providers of financial capital

B   To support integrated thinking and decision making

C   To communicate the impacts of economic, environmental and social and governance performance X

D   To increase the quantity of information available to providers of financial capital

E   To provide a more cohesive and efficient approach to corporate reporting

17   Which THREE of the following are defined by the Global Reporting Initiative as being Principles for Defining Report Content?

Ⓐ   Sustainability context

B   Clarity

C   Comparability

Ⓓ   Materiality

Ⓔ   Completeness

18   If an entity is unable to make all the disclosures as required by the Global Reporting Initiative's (GRI) Sustainability Reporting Standards, which of the following is true?

A   The entity is not allowed to state that its sustainability report has been produced in accordance with the guidelines

Ⓑ   The entity must state what information has been omitted and why it has been omitted

C   The entity must state what information has been omitted, but not necessarily why it has been omitted

D   The entity can still state that the sustainability report has been produced in accordance with the guidelines, without any further disclosure of the information omitted

19   Mountain Co is a well-established manufacturing company with operations in many countries. Its products have an excellent reputation.

In Mountain Co's Integrated Report, how would it present this information?

A   It would not disclose this information explicitly

Ⓑ   As part of its disclosure of social and relationship capitals

C   As part of its disclosure of intellectual capitals

D   As part of its disclosure of manufactured capitals

20   Which of the following statements best describes the link between sustainability reporting and integrated reporting?

A   there is no link between sustainability reporting and integrated reporting

B   sustainability reporting and integrated reporting are the same

C   integrated reporting is an integral part of sustainability reporting

Ⓓ   sustainability reporting is an integral part of integrated reporting

21 Loose Co has prepared a draft Integrated Report following the International Integrated Reporting Council's <IR> Framework.

Which THREE of the headings below have been placed in the wrong section of the report?

Guiding principles

(A) Disclosures on Management Approach

B Strategic focus and future orientation ✓

(C) Risks and opportunities

D Connectivity of information ✓

Content elements

E Organisational overview and external environment ✓

(F) Consistency and comparability

G Strategy and resource allocation ✓

H Performance ✓

22 **Which TWO of the following are most likely to increase the wealth of an all-equity financed entity's shareholders?**

A Paying out a large dividend

(B) Investing in a new project with a positive net present value

C Raising new equity finance to invest in a zero NPV project

(D) Raising new debt finance to invest in a zero NPV project

23 Napoli Co, a manufacturing company, has applied to borrow $1 million from its bank.

Which THREE of the following characteristics of Napoli Co are likely to be viewed positively by the bank?

(A) It has a wide range of well-established products

B Its order book is clear after the next three months ✗

(C) It is all equity financed

(D) It has a good reputation for paying payables on time

E There is a single supplier of raw materials ✗

24 Thursday Co has an AAA credit rating and Cass Co has an A rating.

Enter the correct word from the choices given:

Thursday Co will probably find it _____ (easier/~~harder~~) to raise debt finance than Cass Co.

The rate of interest on borrowings is likely to be _____ (~~higher~~/lower) for Thursday Co than Cass Co.

25 The managers of Green Co are trying to identify the optimum amount of cash to hold.

Enter the correct phrase from the choices given:

Holding _____ (~~too much~~/too little) cash will potentially leave the entity subject to liquidity problems and possible liquidation.

Holding _____ (too much/~~too little~~) cash has an opportunity cost (lost interest on deposits, or returns on attractive investments).

Holding _____ (too much/~~too little~~) cash leaves an entity vulnerable to a takeover bid.

26 **What is the aim of thin capitalisation rules?**

   A   to enable companies to claim tax relief on interest

   B   to allow companies to pay dividends to other companies in a group

   C   to prevent small companies from being subject to hostile takeover bids

   (D)   to prevent companies from getting excessive tax relief on interest

27 Vischer Concrete has $1.2 million in assets that are currently financed with 100% equity finance. Vischer's earnings before interest and tax (EBIT) are $300,000 and its tax rate is 30%.

If Vischer changes its capital structure to include 40% debt, what is Vischer's return on equity (ROE) before and after the change? (Assume that the interest rate on debt is 5%.)

	ROE at 100% equity	*ROE at 60% equity*
A	17.5%	37.5%
B	17.5%	26.8%
C	25.0%	26.8%
D	25.0%	37.5%

28 Audre Co has the following financial objectives:

   •   to achieve an average dividend growth of at least 7% per annum

   •   to keep its gearing, measured as [debt/(debt + equity)] by market value, below 30%

In the last three years, Audre Co's dividend has grown from $0.55 million to $0.70 million.

Audre Co has 2 million $0.50 shares in issue, trading at $1.24, and 10,000 bonds with a par value of $100 and a market value of $105.

Which of the objectives has Audre Co achieved?

   A   Neither objective

   B   Just the gearing objective

   C   Just the dividend growth objective

   D   Both objectives

29   Dunk Co has just reported a profit before interest and tax of $25 million. It has a 6% interest bank loan of $60 million, which carries an interest cover covenant (based on profit before interest and tax) of 4 times.

Dunk Co plans to borrow an additional $40 million, at 5% interest, from another bank to finance a new investment project.

What is the likely interest cover if the new finance is raised, and is the covenant likely to be breached?

	Interest cover	Covenant
A	4.46	Breached
B	4.46	Not breached
C	6.94	Breached
D	6.94	Not breached

30   Thiago Co is a UK based company that makes sales to US customers. It generated revenue of USD 1.50 million last year and its cost of sales was GBP 0.67 million. The exchange rate at the year-end was GBP/USD 1.6500 (that is GBP 1 = USD 1.6500).

In the coming year, selling prices are expected to increase by 4% and sales volumes are expected to stay constant.

If the exchange rate is likely to stay constant, what will Thiago Co's gross profit margin be in the coming year?

A   26.3%

B   29.1%

C   55.3%

D   57.1%

31   Which of the following best describes the relationship between sustainability reporting (e.g. using the GRI Standards) and integrated reporting (e.g. using the <IR> Framework)?

A   Sustainability reporting and integrated reporting are the same thing

B   Sustainability reporting and integrated reporting are unrelated

C   Integrated reporting forms part of sustainability reporting

D   Sustainability reporting forms part of integrated reporting

32   Demarcus is the CFO of a large international quoted company. He is interested in preparing an integrated report, rather than just the usual statutory financial statements.

Which one of the following is NOT an advantage of preparing an integrated report?

A   It will help ensure the organisation meets its legal requirements to provide integrated information

B   It will provide more information to stakeholders and potential investors

C   It will provide strategic insight and detailed information for management

D   It will help ensure management focus on both financial and non-financial objectives

33 Cleo is a charity focussed on providing support and accommodation to homeless people in their local region. Cleo has a mix of financial and non-financial objectives.

Which of the following will NOT improve value for money?

A Minimising the amount of time that the Cleo's properties are unoccupied

B Negotiating bulk discounts on building supplies

C Obtaining more low cost accommodation

D Focussing on maintaining a healthy surplus every year

SYLLABUS SECTION B: SOURCES OF LONG-TERM FUNDS

34 **Modigliani and Miller's 1963 gearing theory concludes that:**

A There is an optimum gearing level at which the cost of capital is maximised

B The cost of capital reduces as the gearing level increases

C The cost of capital increases as the gearing level increases

D There is an optimum gearing level at which the cost of capital is minimised

35 **The traditional view of gearing concludes that:**

A The value of the company reduces as the gearing level increases

B The value of the company increases as the gearing level increases

C There is an optimum gearing level at which the value of the company is maximised

D There is an optimum gearing level at which the value of the company is minimised

36 XX Co is a geared company whose equity has a market value of $1,350 million and debt has a market value of $420 million.

XX Co plans to issue $200 million of new shares, and to use the funds raised to pay off some of the debt.

XX Co currently has a cost of equity of 13.5%, and YY Co (an equivalent ungeared company operating in the same business sector as XX Co) has a cost of equity of 12.8%.

XX Co's WACC is currently 11.9% and the tax rate is 30%.

According to Modigliani and Miller's theory with tax, XX Co's WACC will move to:

A $$12.3\% = 12.8\% \times \left[1 - \left(\frac{0.30 \times 220}{1,710} \right) \right]$$

B $$13.0\% = 13.5\% \times \left[1 - \left(\frac{0.30 \times 220}{1,770} \right) \right]$$

C $$12.3\% = 12.8\% \times \left[1 - \left(\frac{0.30 \times 220}{1,770} \right) \right]$$

D $$13.0\% = 13.5\% \times \left[1 - \left(\frac{0.30 \times 220}{1,710} \right) \right]$$

37 **ZZZ is an ungeared company with a cost of equity of 10%. It is considering issuing some bonds, so that its gearing level will be 20% debt and 80% equity. The bonds will pay a coupon rate of 5%, and the <u>yield required by the lenders will be 6%.</u>**

If ZZZ pays tax at 25%, according to Modigliani and Miller's theory with tax, ZZZ's cost of equity will move to:

A $11.25\% = 10\% + [(10\% - 5\%) \times (^{20}\!/\!_{80})]$

B $10.75\% = 10\% + [(10\% - 6\%) \times (^{15}\!/\!_{80})]$

C $10.94\% = 10\% + [(10\% - 5\%) \times (^{15}\!/\!_{80})]$

D $11.00\% = 10\% + [(10\% - 6\%) \times (^{20}\!/\!_{80})]$

10+10

$\dfrac{15}{80}$

38 Monty is an all-equity financed company with a cost of equity of 15%.

The directors of Monty are proposing to raise $20 million to invest in a new project. This investment will carry similar risk to Monty's current business. It is proposed that the investment will be financed by either

- a rights issue of shares, or

- an issue of an undated bond carrying 6% interest pre-tax (this rate is deemed to reflect the returns required by the market for the risk and duration of the bond).

Earnings for Monty are forecast to be $30 million in the first year after the new investment. Subsequently, earnings are expected to remain at a constant level each year.

The corporate income tax rate is 20%. This is not expected to change.

According to Modigliani and Miller's theory with tax, the value of Monty's EQUITY if it issues the bond and undertakes this project will be:

A $204 million

B $200 million

C $184 million

D $180 million

$V_g = V_u + TB$

$30/.15$

$200 \quad .2 \times 20$

$204 = 200 + 164$

(20)

184

$15\% + (15 - 6\%)\dfrac{16}{}$

39

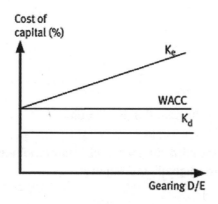

According to Modigliani and Miller's <u>1958</u> model of capital market efficiency, why is the cost of debt (Kd) lower than the cost of equity (Ke)?

A   Interest is received more regularly than dividends

B   Dividend tax credits are received by investors

C   Interest returns are more reliable than dividends

D   Interest is tax deductible   ✗

40   C Co is identical in all operating and risk characteristics to D Co, but their capital structures differ:

C Co: $72 million equity only

D Co: $36.2 million debt, 10 million shares

The tax rate is 33%.

What is the value of D Co's equity per share?

A $47.746 million

B $3.58

C $4.77

D $7.20

41   A Co is identical in all operating and risk characteristics to B Co, but their capital structures differ.

B Co is financed only by equity, currently valued at $37.2 million.

A Co has equity : debt 2:1 as its capital structure.

A Co's pre-tax cost of debt is 7.5%, and B Co's cost of equity is 17.5%.

A Co and B Co both operate in a country where tax is payable at 33%.

What is the cost of equity for A Co (to 2 decimal places)?

A   20.85%

B   13.06%

C   22.50%

D   7.77%

42   According to Modigliani and Miller the cost of equity will always fall with decreased gearing because:

A   The firm is less likely to go bankrupt

B   Debt is allowable against tax   ✗

C   The return to shareholders becomes less variable

D   The tax shield on debt increases the value of the shareholders' equity   ✗

43   **Which one of the following diagrams is consistent with the so-called 'traditional view' of gearing often held in contrast with the views of Modigliani and Miller?**

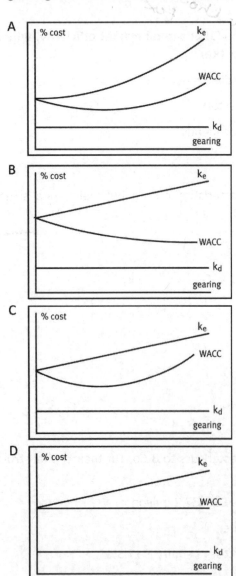

44   Cork currently has a gearing ratio of 20% (based on market values and measured as debt/ (debt + equity) and a WACC of 9.4%. The corporate income tax rate is 30%.

Calculate, using Modigliani and Miller's theory with tax, the theoretical WACC for Cork if gearing were to be increased to 40%.

Enter your answer as a percentage to one decimal place.

(INSERT CORRECT FIGURE IN THE BOX)

45   Davis is an all equity financed company with a market value of $60m and a cost of capital of 15% per annum. The corporation tax rate is 30%.

If the company repurchases $20m of equity and replaces it with 6% undated bonds, what will be the company's new WACC?

A   11.4%

B   12.0%

C   13.5%

D   13.6%

46   Lallana is an all equity financed company with an ungeared cost of equity of 15%. They have been advised that if the company were to issue debt and use the funds to repurchase shares it would lower the company's WACC. The corporation tax rate is 30%.

If the Board would like to reduce WACC by 1%, what would be the required gearing ratio (measured as debt/(debt + equity) using market values) to achieve this?

Enter your answer as a percentage to two decimal places.

(INSERT CORRECT FIGURE IN THE BOX)

47   Schneiderlin currently has a gearing ratio of 20% (based on market values and measured as debt/(debt + equity) and a WACC of 9.4%. The corporation tax rate is 30%.

Calculate, using Modigliani and Miller's theory with tax, the relative percentage change in WACC for Schneiderlin plc if gearing were to be increased to 40%.

Enter your answer as a percentage to one decimal place.

(INSERT CORRECT FIGURE IN THE BOX)

48   Wanyama has 20m equity shares in issue trading at 260 cents per share and an 8% bank loan of $8m. The corporation tax rate is 30%. The Board are considering issuing more shares in order to pay off the bank loan but are unsure of the impact it will have on the company's WACC. The company's cost of equity is currently 14%.

Calculate the new WACC if the Board's proposal goes ahead.

(INSERT CORRECT FIGURE IN THE BOX)

49   YrElen Co is currently all equity financed and has a cost of capital of 15%. It is considering changing its capital structure by issuing, at par, long dated bonds with a coupon rate of 5%. It plans to have a debt to equity ratio of 1 to 4. The company pays tax at 20%.

What will be the resultant Weighted Average Cost of Capital (WACC)?

| |
| |

(INSERT CORRECT FIGURE IN THE BOX, rounded to 1 decimal place of a % point)

50   Ygarn Co is currently financed by $100 million of equity shares and $40 million of debt. Its cost of equity is 14% and the pre-tax cost of debt is 8%. It pays tax at a rate of 20%.

What would the cost of equity change to if the company changed its debt to equity ratio to 60%?

| |
| |

(INSERT CORRECT FIGURE IN THE BOX, rounded to 1 decimal place of a % point)

51   GlyderFawr Co is currently all equity financed with 10 million shares in issue. The shares have a current market value of $9.50 each. The company is considering issuing $20 million of debt and using the proceeds to re-purchase some of its own equity shares (at market value). It pays corporation tax at 20%

What would be the market value, per share, of the remaining equity shares?

| |
| |

(INSERT CORRECT FIGURE IN THE BOX, in $ to 2 decimal places)

52   **Which of the following is a difference between primary and secondary capital markets?**

A   Both primary and secondary markets relate to where shares and bonds trade after their initial offering

B   Secondary capital markets relate to the sale of new issues of bonds, preference shares, and ordinary shares, while primary capital markets are where securities trade after their initial offering

C   Primary capital markets relate to the sale of new issues of bonds, preference shares, and ordinary shares, while secondary capital markets are where securities trade after their initial offering.

D   Primary markets are where shares trade while secondary markets are where bonds trade

53   **Enter the correct word from the choices given:**

Company X has two covenants attached to its borrowings:

• The interest cover ratio must be _____ **(higher/lower)** than 3

• The ratio of net debt to EBITDA must be _____ **(higher/lower)** than 3

54 A company has issued tradable bonds which have a covenant attached. The covenant does not allow the gearing ratio (as measured by debt divided by equity, calculated on market values) to exceed 45%. If the covenant is breached, then the bonds become immediately re-payable.

This morning, the share price fell to $1.75. The company has 1m shares in issue. It also has $0.4m of bank loans and $0.5m (nominal) of bonds. The bonds are currently trading at $88 per $100 nominal.

Has the covenant been breached and if so, what action must be taken immediately to try to bring it back into line to avoid having to repay the bonds?

A   Covenant breached – yes. Release news about lucrative, new projects

B   Covenant breached – yes. Borrow more from the bank to increase liquidity

C   Covenant breached – yes. Launch a share re-purchase scheme

D   Covenant breached – no. No action required

55 Alice Co is financed partly by equity shares and partly by a $50 million bank borrowing with a fixed interest rate of 10%. The bank borrowing carries a covenant that requires the company to keep its annual retained earnings to $5 million or more.

The company recently invested in a large new investment project which has significantly increased the annual earnings. The project was funded by a rights issue of shares, so the directors are keen to reward the shareholders for their investment by paying a large one-off dividend.

Assuming that the current year's profit before interest and tax is $30 million, and that the rate of corporate income tax is 20%, which of the following represents the maximum dividend that the company will be able to pay without breaching the covenant?

A $15 million, being [$30 million – (10% × $50 million)] × 80%, minus the $5 million retained earnings limit

B $19 million, being ($30 million × 80%), minus the $5 million retained earnings limit

C $20 million, being [$30 million – (10% × $50 million)], minus the $5 million retained earnings limit

D $25 million, being $30 million minus the $5 million retained earnings limit

56 Sansa Co is looking to acquire a new piece of machinery. If buying, the machine will cost $1m and will attract capital allowances on a reducing balance basis at 25% per annum. The life of the machine is expected to be four years with no residual value. If it is leased, the lease payments will be $275,000 in advance each year.

Sansa Co can borrow from its bank at 8.57% per annum and pays tax at 30% one year in arrears. If leasing, the full lease payment will qualify for tax relief.

What is the present value of the lease payments (to the nearest '000)?

A   ($759,000)

B   ($740,000)

C   ($502,000)

D $11,000

See notes

57   Company S is considering acquiring an asset which will cost $450,000 to purchase outright. However S is exploring a lease arrangement. The lessor will charge $120,000 per annum in arrears for four years. Tax relief is available in the year in which profits are earned at 30%. Only the interest element of the lease payment will attract tax relief.

Using the sum of the digits method, what is the tax relief on the interest paid in year 3?

A $6,000

B $2,700

C $1,800

D $900

Handwritten annotations:
Asset 450

120×4 = 480
          ‾‾‾‾
          450
          ‾‾‾‾
          30

4(4+1)/2 = 10

1 4/10
2 3/10
3 2/10 ×30 = 6000 ×3 =
4 1/10   = 1800

58   Bran Co is considering whether to lease or buy an asset.

The financial controller has been researching the costs involved with borrowing from the bank to buy the asset outright. The bank will charge interest at 7.14% per annum. The asset will cost $500,000 and will attract tax allowable depreciation on a straight line basis over five years, which is the useful economic life of the asset. There is no residual value.

Bran Co is subject to corporation tax at 30%, payable in the year in which the profit is earned.

To the nearest $000, what is the NPV of the buy option?

[   ]   (INSERT CORRECT FIGURE IN THE BOX)

59   V Co is a company whose directors are considering an Initial Public Offering (IPO) of shares.

The directors are hoping to generate a large amount of cash for the company, so they intend to appoint an advisor to organise the IPO.

Who should the directors appoint to organise the IPO?

A   an underwriter

B   a stockbroker

C   an investment bank

D   an institutional investor

60   A company makes a 1 for 5 rights issue at a price of $3.50. The cum-rights price is $5.

What is the theoretical ex-rights price?

A $3.75

B $4.25

C $4.70

D $4.75

61 A company currently has 15 million $1 shares in issue with a market value of $5 per share. The company wishes to raise new funds using a 1 for 3 rights issue.

If the theoretical ex rights price per share turns out to be $4.80, how much new finance was raised?

A $21 million

B $24 million

C $207 million

D $213 million

62 **The main reason for discounting a rights issue is:**

A To make the shares attractive to shareholders

B To counteract the dilution of owner's equity

C To safeguard against the risk of a fall in market price during the offer period

D To return value to existing shareholders

63 An all equity financed company is about to raise the finance for a new project by an issue of ordinary shares to the general public. The new project has a positive Net Present Value (NPV).

If all the gain from the new project is to go to the existing shareholders, which of the following statements about the issue price (per share) of the new shares is true?

A It must be equal to the nominal value of the share issued

B It must be equal to the current market value of an existing share

C It must be at a discount to the current market value of an existing share

D It must be greater than the current market value of an existing share

64 Snowdon Co is financed entirely by equity comprising 10 million ordinary shares with a current market value of $5 per share. It is planning to make an issue of new ordinary shares to the general public in order to raise the funds to invest in a new project which will cost $5.28 million, and will give a positive NPV of $1.885 million. The issue will be priced at a 4% discount to the current share price.

What (to the nearest $) will be the total gain accruing to the existing shareholders?

[   ] (INSERT CORRECT FIGURE IN THE BOX)

65 CribGoch Co is financed entirely by equity comprising 10 million ordinary shares with a current market value of $5 per share.

It is planning to make an issue of new ordinary shares to the general public in order to raise the funds to invest in a new project which will cost $5.28 million, and will give a positive NPV of $2.44 million.

The issue will be priced at a 4% discount to the current share price.

What percentage (to 2 decimal places) of the total gain will go to the new shareholders?

[   ] (INSERT CORRECT FIGURE IN THE BOX)

66   Tryfan Co intends to invest $8 million in a new project with an NPV of $3 million. The company is currently financed entirely by 30 million shares with a market value of $2.50 per share. The funds for the new project will be raised by issuing new ordinary shares to a private investor.

What price should the new shares be issued at if all the gain is to go to the existing shareholders?

[   ] (INSERT CORRECT FIGURE IN THE BOX)

67   GlyderFach Co is financed entirely by equity comprising 20 million ordinary shares with a current market value of $3.50 per share. It is planning to make an issue of new ordinary shares to the general public at a discount of 10% to the current market price in order to raise the funds to invest in a new project. The new project will cost $2.835 million and generates a positive Net Present Value of $1.151 million.

What is the gain per share for the new investors?

[   ] (INSERT CORRECT FIGURE IN THE BOX)

68   **Which of the following is the best statement of the conclusion of Modigliani and Miller on the relevance of dividend policy?**

   A   All shareholders are indifferent between receiving dividend income and capital gains

   B   Increase in retentions results in a higher growth rate

   C   The value of the shareholders' equity is determined solely by the firm's investment selection criteria

   D   Discounting the dividends is not an appropriate way to value the firm's equity

69   Some companies have a long-term dividend policy of paying out no dividends. A notable example has been Microsoft, the US software corporation.

Which of the following is the weakest and least likely reason for justifying a no-dividend policy over the long term?

   A   Retained profits are a cheaper source of new finance than raising new debt capital in the markets

   B   The tax treatment of capital gains is more favourable than the tax treatment of dividends

   C   Shareholders needing cash can sell shares in the stock market at any time, and so do not need dividends

   D   The company is a growth company and investors buying shares in the company recognise that all profits will be reinvested for growth

70   According to Modigliani and Miller's dividend irrelevancy theory, investors are indifferent as to whether they receive a dividend or capital growth in their share value as they can manufacture their own dividend by selling shares.

Which THREE of the following are reasons why an investor might disagree with this theory?

(A)   Transaction costs may apply when selling shares

(B)   Tax planning will be affected

C   Share price will fall if no dividends are paid

D   The investor is reliant on the cash dividend

(E)   The investor's ability to influence management will be reduced

71   According to Modigliani and Miller's 1963 'with tax' model, interest costs are cheaper for a company to finance than dividend costs?

Select TWO reasons why from the following list.

A   Dividends are paid out of post-tax earnings

B   Debt is secured on specific assets   ✗

C   Interest returns are guaranteed

D   Dividends can be reduced if company performance is weak ✗

E   Lower transaction costs

72   Cazorla Co has paid a reliable dividend in recent years. It is considering reducing its dividend to conserve cash.

Cazorla Co's share price is likely to fall due to which THREE of the following reasons?

(A)   Disappointed investors selling shares   *Clientele*

B   Low returns earned on conserved cash

C   Poor performance of the business relative to other companies

(D)   Investors selling shares to replace lost dividends   *Bird in Hand*

(E)   Negative market perception of company performance   *Signalling*

73   **Enter the correct word from the choices given:**

Company X is planning on _____ **(increasing/decreasing)** its dividend, but is concerned that the share price will fall.

This demonstrates the _____ **(signalling/clientele)** effect.

74   Popov Co currently has 10 million $0.50 ordinary shares in issue, trading at $1.93.

A proposed new project is expected to have a net present value of $6 million and requires an initial investment of $5 million. The project's internal rate of return is expected to be 9%.

If the market is efficient and the share price moves to reflect this information on the day that the project is announced, what is the theoretical movement in the share price on that day?

A $0.60 increase

B $0.10 increase

C $0.50 decrease

D   No change

75   PP Co made an operating profit of $305,000 last year, and its directors are considering issuing $500,000 of new secured bonds at their par value of $100. The coupon rate will be 2.5%.

PP Co is a listed company. It currently has 1 million $0.50 shares in issue, trading at $0.95, and 10,000, 4% coupon bonds with par value $100 and market value $95.

What will be the interest cover of PP Co in the year after the bonds are issued, on the assumption that operating profits will stay constant?

A   5.8

B   6.0

C   8.1

D   18.5

76   Lung Co has a debt covenant that requires its gearing ratio (measured as debt/(debt + equity) using market values) to be less than 35%, and its interest cover to be greater than 2.2

Extracts from its recent financial statements show that it has 200,000 $1 shares in issue and it has a 9% interest bank loan of $100,000. It made a profit before interest and tax last year of $25,000.

The current share price is $1.30 per share.

The directors of Lung Co are considering borrowing an extra $40,000 from the bank as a secured loan at an interest rate of 5% per annum.

Annual profits are expected to stay constant, but the share price is expected to fall to $1.25 per share to reflect the shareholders' perception of increased financial risk.

Assuming the new finance is raised, which of the following shows Grass Co's position with regard to its debt covenant:

	Gearing	Interest cover
A	MET	MET
B	FAILED	MET
C	FAILED	FAILED
D	MET	FAILED

77   Na Co currently has a cash balance of $5 million and earnings per share of $0.30.

It has 6 million $0.25 shares in issue, but the directors are planning to repurchase 1 million of these shares at a price of $0.40 each.

What will be the cash balance and the earnings per share (EPS) after the share repurchase?

	Cash	EPS
A	$3.0 million	$0.36
B	$4.6 million	$0.36
C	$3.0 million	$0.25
D	$4.6 million	$0.25

78   The directors of Strange Co are considering using either a 6% interest bank loan, or issuing 250,000 ordinary shares at a price of $4, to raise necessary funds for expansion.

The expansion will generate $300,000 of extra operating profit each year.

Strange Co pays tax at 30%.

Key investor ratios for Strange Co are currently as follows:

Interest cover = (Earnings before interest and tax/Interest payable) = $1,300,000/$280,000 = 4.6 times

Earnings per share (EPS) = (Profit after tax/No. of shares) = $714,000/1,000,000 = $0.714

Gearing = (debt/equity) = $4m/$7m = 57.1%

Which TWO of the following statements are correct?

A   Gearing falls when using equity and rises when using debt

B   EPS increases more by using debt

C   Equity reduces gearing and gives the best EPS

D   EPS and interest cover both worsen using debt

E   Interest cover is reduced using either source of finance

79   After several years of growth, Goose Co has accumulated a cash pile of $10 million. The directors have decided to repurchase some of the company's shares at market value in order to return this cash pile to the shareholders.

Goose Co has 40 million $1 shares in issue, trading at $3.14. It also has $50 million of bonds in issue, trading at $99 per cent.

What will be the gearing level of Goose Co after the share repurchase? (measured as debt/(debt + equity) using market values)

A   26.7%

B   28.3%

C   30.0%

D   62.5%

80 The directors of Singh Co are considering raising $500,000 in order to undertake a new project. It is expected that the new project will cause earnings to rise by $50,000 each year. Singh Co has 2 million $0.50 shares in issue, which are currently trading at $0.90. Singh Co's P/E ratio is 8.55.

If Singh Co uses a 1 for 2 rights issue to raise the finance, what is the expected earnings per share (EPS) of Singh Co after the finance has been raised and the project undertaken?

A $0.500

B $0.105

C $0.087

D $0.050

81 Tide Co is a listed company. Its $1 ordinary shares are quoted on the local stock exchange.

The Board of Tide Co is aware that the market is expecting Tide Co to pay a dividend of $100m to be paid at the year end, but in order to fund the investment in an important new project, the Board is considering offering a scrip dividend of 1 share for every 10 shares held instead of a cash dividend.

Profit after tax and interest is forecast to be $290 million in the current financial year, and Tide Co's equity comprises:

Ordinary share capital ($1 shares) $1,000m

Reserves $400m

Tide Co's share price is $1.65 per share.

What is the expected share price of Tide Co after the scrip dividend has been issued? (to 2 decimal places)

A $1.82

B $1.65

C $1.50

D $0.17

82 UU Co is considering raising $3 million of new long term debt finance to fund the acquisition of Ping Co.

Ping Co is considered to have a value to UU Co of $3.6 million. UU Co's most recent statement of financial position shows long term borrowings of $6.2 million, share capital ($1 shares) of $4 million and accumulated reserves of $6.1 million. The current market share price for UU Co is $3.08 per share.

What will be the gearing ratio – measured as (debt/(debt + equity)) at book value – after the acquisition?

A   47.7%

B   46.2%

C   42.8%

D   41.6%

83 **Statement of financial position for Shadows Co**

	$m
Non-current assets (total)	28.0
Current assets (total)	25.0
TOTAL ASSETS	53.0
Equity and Liabilities	
Ordinary share capital	20.0
Ordinary share premium	4.0
Preference share capital (irredeemable)	5.0
Reserves	6.0
Non-current liabilities	
10% bonds	10.0
Current liabilities	
Trade creditors	3.0
Bank overdraft	5.0
TOTAL EQUITY & LIABILITIES	53.0

Shadows Co statement of profit or loss extract	$m
Operating profit (PBIT)	8.3
Finance charges	(1.0)
Profit before tax (PBT)	7.3
Tax @ 30%	(2.2)
Net profit	5.1

Shadows Co is considering raising additional debt finance of $8m. The interest rate on the new debt will be 8% per annum. Operating profit is expected to stay constant after the new finance has been raised.

What will be the interest cover and the capital gearing ratio (measured as debt/(debt + equity) at book value and including the overdraft as part of debt) for Shadows Co after the new finance has been raised?

A   Interest cover 5.06, gearing 39.7%

B   Interest cover 5.06, gearing 53.5%

C   Interest cover 12.97, gearing 39.7%

D   Interest cover 12.97, gearing 53.5%

SYLLABUS SECTION C: FINANCIAL RISKS

84 **If the exchange rate moves from EUR 1 = USD 0.95 to EUR 1 = USD 1.10, then the euro has:**

    A   depreciated and Europeans will find US goods cheaper

    B   appreciated and Europeans will find US goods more expensive

    C   appreciated and Europeans will find US goods cheaper

    D   depreciated and Europeans will find US goods more expensive

85 **For which of the following reasons do exchange rates fluctuate? Select all that apply.**

    A   Changes in the balance of payments

    B   Government policy

    C   Developments in Information Technology

    D   Speculation

    E   Capital movements between economies

86 'There is a risk that the value of our foreign currency-denominated assets and liabilities will change when we prepare our accounts.'

    To which risk does the above statement refer?

    A   Translation risk

    B   Economic risk

    C   Transaction risk

    D   Interest rate risk

87 Eady Co is a UK company that imports furniture from a Canadian supplier and sells it throughout Europe. Eady Co has just received a shipment of furniture, invoiced in Canadian dollars, for which payment is to be made in two months' time. Neither Eady Co nor the Canadian supplier use hedging techniques to cover their exchange risk.

    If the British Pound were to weaken substantially against the Canadian dollar, what would be the foreign exchange gain or loss effects upon Eady Co and the Canadian supplier?

	Eady Co	*Canadian supplier*
A	Gain	No effect
B	No effect	Gain
C	Loss	No effect
D	Loss	Gain

88   **Political risk analysis is conducted by a company considering international operations and normally focuses on the:**

   A   world economy generally

   B   relations between the USA, Japan and Europe

   C   political and cultural differences between the home and target country

   D   industrialisation of the target country

89   **The interest rate risk of a bond is the:**

   A   risk related to the possibility of bankruptcy of the bond's issuer

   B   unsystematic risk caused by factors unique in the bond

   C   risk related to the possibility of bankruptcy of the bond's issuer that arises from the uncertainty of the bond's return caused by the change in interest rates

   D   risk that arises from the uncertainty about the bond's return caused by changes in interest rates over time

90   **If Brewer Corporation's bonds are currently yielding 8% in the marketplace, why would the entity's cost of debt be lower?**

   A   Additional debt can be issued more cheaply than the original debt

   B   Market interest rates have increased

   C   There should be no difference; cost of debt is the same as the bonds' market yield

   D   Interest is deductible for tax purposes

91   **Company P has decided to finance its foreign investment through local finance. Which of the following statements is correct? Select all that apply.**

   A   Local financing can minimise translation risk

   B   Local financing can minimise transaction risk

   C   Local financing can minimise interest rate risk ✗

   D   Local financing is dependent on the state of the banking and capital markets of the country concerned

   E   Local financing reduces the risk of P's assets being confiscated

92   Hannah Co is based in country H, where the functional currency is the H$.

   The spot rate for the H$ to the euro (EUR) is H$ 1 = EUR 6.250.

   The expected interest rates in the Eurozone and country H respectively are 2% and 6% over the next year.

   What is the forecast forward rate of exchange in one year's time using the interest rate parity theory?

   A   H$1 = EUR 6.014

   B   H$1 = EUR 2.083

   C   H$1 = EUR 6.495

   D   H$1 = EUR 18.750

93   Jo Co has suppliers and customers in many different countries around the world, so the directors of Jo Co monitor movements in exchange rates closely, using interest rate parity theory to estimate the likely future exchange rates.

The current exchange rate between the British pound (GBP) and the euro (EUR) is GBP 1 = EUR 1.2400, and the expected interest rates in the UK and the Eurozone respectively are 0.5% and 0.75% over the next year.

What is the forecast forward rate of exchange in one year's time using the interest rate parity theory?

A   GBP 1 = EUR 1.2112

B   GBP 1 = EUR 1.2369

C   GBP 1 = EUR 1.2431

D   GBP 1 = EUR 1.2695

94   The current exchange rate between the British pound (GBP) and the euro (EUR) is GBP 1 = EUR 1.2075, and the GBP is expected to appreciate by approximately 2% per year over the next few years.

What is the expected rate of exchange in two years' time?

A   GBP 1 = EUR 1.2317

B   GBP 1 = EUR 1.2563

C   GBP 1 = EUR 1.1838

D   GBP 1 = EUR 1.1606

95   W Co is based in country W (functional currency W$) and it makes some purchases from the Eurozone, denominated in euros (EUR). Purchases in 1 year's time are expected to be EUR 100,000. The financial director of W Co is attempting to estimate the likely exchange rate in 1 year's time, so that she can assess the likely value of the entity's foreign currency expenditure.

The spot rate of exchange is W$ 1 = EUR 1.9900. Interest rates in the Eurozone and country W are expected to be 1% and 8% respectively over the next year.

What is the expected spot in 1 year's time, using interest rate parity, and what is the expected value of the EUR sales when translated into W$?

	Exchange rate	Value of expenditure
A	W$1 = EUR 2.1279	W$ 212,792
B	W$1 = EUR 2.1279	W$ 46,995
C	W$1 = EUR 1.8610	W$ 186,100
D	W$1 = EUR 1.8610	W$ 53,735

96 CC Co is based in country C (functional currency C$) and it makes some sales in the USA, denominated in US dollars (USD).

The spot rate of exchange is C$ 1 = USD 1.1144. Interest rates in the USA and country C are expected to be 3% and 5% respectively over the next few years.

What is the expected rate of exchange in 6 months' time, using interest rate parity theory?

A   C$1 = USD 1.1252

B   C$1 = USD 1.0932

C   C$1 = USD 1.1037

D   C$1 = USD 1.1360

97 Interest Rate Parity Theory generally holds true in practice. However it suffers from several limitations.

Which of the following is not a limitation of Interest Rate Parity Theory?

A   Government controls on capital markets

B   Controls on currency trading

C   Intervention in foreign exchange markets

D   Future inflation rates are only estimates

98 In Country A inflation is predicted to be 5% and (nominal) interest rates are 11.3%. In Country B interest rates are 13.42%.

Assuming the International Fisher effect holds, determine the expected inflation rate in Country B. (Give your answer as a percentage to 1 decimal place)

_____

99 X is a bank. The management accountant of X has estimated that the value of its asset portfolio at year end will be $1,200 million, with a standard deviation of $430 million.

Calculate the value at risk of the portfolio, at a 95% confidence level. (Express your answer in $, rounded to the nearest million.)

$ _____

100 Biskit Co, a UK based company, has sold goods on credit to an American customer. It has invoiced in dollars (USD) for 10 million.

The exchange rate is currently USD 1.2785 to GBP 1.

The daily volatility of the exchange rate is 0.75%.

Calculate to the nearest GBP 1,000, the 1-day 97.5% VAR.

GBP _____

Calculate to the nearest GBP 1,000, the 5-day 97.5% VAR.

GBP _____

101   Edted is a UK company that has to pay a Spanish supplier EUR 100,000 in three months' time. The company's Finance Director wishes to avoid exchange rate exposure, and is looking at four options.

(1)   Do nothing for three months and then buy Euros at the spot rate.

(2)   Pay in full now, buying Euros at today's spot rate.

(3)   Buy Euros now, put them on deposit for three months, and pay the debt with these Euros plus accumulated interest.

(4)   Arrange a forward exchange contract to buy the euros in three months' time.

Which of these options would provide cover against the exchange rate exposure that Edted would otherwise suffer?

A   Option (4) only

B   Options (3) and (4) only

C   Options (2), (3) and (4) only

D   Options (1), (2), (3) and (4)

102   Methods for hedging foreign currency risk can be classified as either 'internal' or 'external'. Drag and drop the following hedging methods into the correct category.

	Internal	External
Forward contracts		
Futures		
Leading and lagging		
Matching and netting		
Options		
Countertrade		

103   There are different methods that can be used to internally hedge foreign exchange risk. Match the examples below to the appropriate method.

Method	Example
Matching	Transferring all bank account balances in one currency into a single account
Netting	Exchanging goods or services of similar value
Pooling	Financing a foreign investment with a foreign currency loan
Countertrade	Using a foreign currency receipt to offset a foreign currency payment

104 The following options are held by Frances Co at their expiry date:

(1) A call option on GBP 500,000 in exchange for USD at an exercise price of GBP 1 = USD 1.90. The exchange rate at the expiry date is GBP 1 = USD 1.95.

(2) A put option on GBP 400,000 in exchange for Singapore Dollars at an exercise price of GBP 1 = SGD 2.90. The exchange rate at the expiry date is GBP 1 = SGD 2.95.

Which one of the following combinations (exercise/lapse) should be undertaken by the company?

	Call	Put
A	Exercise	Lapse
B	Exercise	Exercise
C	Lapse	Exercise
D	Lapse	Lapse

105 SGB Co in the UK has sold USD 5 million worth of goods to a US customer. The company is considering hedging the contract using options.

The current spot rate is USD 1.5500 to GBP 1 and the option strike price is USD 1.6000 to GBP 1. The contract size is GBP 25,000 per contract and the premium is USD 1,000 per contract.

What is the GBP value of the premium that SGB must pay?

A 80,645

B 83,226

C 125,000

D 129,000

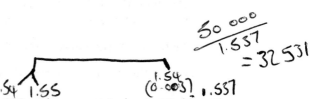

106 X (a UK company) has purchased goods for USD 50,000 and payment is due in 30 days. The current spot rate is USD 1.5400 – 1.5500 to GBP 1 and the one month forward contract is priced at 0.30 – 0.50 cents premium.

Calculate the amount of GBP that X will pay under the forward contract (to the nearest GBP).

GBP 32531

107 X (a UK company) must pay EUR 1 million to a Spanish supplier in six months' time. The treasurer of X has obtained the following information:

- Spot rate is EUR 1.2000 – 1.1950 to GBP 1

- EUR borrowing can be obtained at 4.0% per year and deposits pay 2.0% per year

- GBP borrowing can be obtained at 5.0% per year and deposits pay 3.0% per year

Calculate the cost to X in GBP of a money market hedge, to the nearest GBP 1,000.

GBP 849000

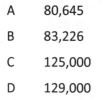

108 DWTV, a US company, has purchased goods from TT Co in the UK at a cost of GBP 25 million.

DWTV has taken out an option at a strike price of GBP 1 = 1.6700 USD with a premium of USD 85,000. When the contract is closed out the spot rate is 1.6850.

What is the USD cost of the purchase to DWTV?

$ _____

109 SOMH, a company based in the United States, is to receive EUR 700,000 from Pops Co (based in Germany) in 6 months' time. The treasurer of SOMH intends to use the forward market to hedge the risk exposure on the transaction.

The spot rate is EUR 1.7027 – 1.6231 to USD 1.

The 6 months forward rate is priced at 2.50 – 1.50 cdis.

How much will SOMH receive in USD, using a forward contract?

A   435,296.31

B   427,324.34

C   417,237.89

D   405,162.93

110 APS is based in the UK, and it has recently sold a significant amount of goods to RJS in France. APS has agreed to invoice in EUR and the total invoice amount is EUR 1,200,000. APS is concerned that the value of the GBP will fluctuate so it has taken out an option at a strike price of GBP 1= EUR 1.4405 and a premium of GBP 35,000.

When the transaction is closed, the spot rate is GBP 1 = 1.4640.

What is the net value in GBP of the contract to APS (to the nearest GBP)?

GBP _____

111 EFG, a UK company, has sold USD 4,000,000 worth of goods to HIJ in the USA. The spot rate is USD 1.2750 to GBP 1, whilst the option strike price is USD 1.4500 to GBP 1. The contract size is GBP 25,000 and the premium is USD 2,500 per contract. EFG has a policy of rounding up when deciding how many contracts to use.

What is the premium in GBP that EFG must pay to set up an option contract?

A   GBP 277,500

B   GBP 215,686

C   GBP 247,059

D   GBP 217,647

112 When hedging interest rate risk, a variety of instruments are available. Match the instruments below with the relevant descriptions.

Instrument		Description
A	Forward Rate Agreement (FRA)	A traded instrument, hedging only downside risk
B	Interest Rate Guarantee (IRG)	A traded instrument, with a fixed rate
C	Future	An over the counter instrument, with a fixed rate
D	Option	An over the counter instrument, hedging only downside risk

113 X (a company) wishes to borrow $1 million in three months, for a period of six months. A bank has quoted the following Forward Rate Agreement (FRA) rates:

3 v 9   5.55 – 5.70

X can borrow at 0.50% above base rate, and the base rate is currently 4.50%. Concerned that base rates may rise, X decides to take the FRA offered by the bank.

At the settlement date for the FRA, base rate has risen to 6.00%. What is the effective interest rate paid by X, for its borrowing? (Answer in %, to 2 decimal places).

|_____| %

114 The owner of an interest-rate cap will

   A   receive a payment if the market rate exceeds the cap rate

   B   receive a payment if the market rate is less than the cap rate

   C   be required to make a payment if the market rate exceeds the cap rate

   D   be required to make a payment if the market rate is less than the cap rate

115 Most futures contracts are closed through which ONE of the following:

   A   delivery

   B   arbitrage

   C   a reversing trade

   D   an exchange-for-physicals

116 Which one of the following statements regarding Over-the-Counter derivatives is true?

   A   They carry no default risk

   B   They are customized contracts

   C   They are backed by the OTC Clearing House

   D   They have good liquidity in the over-the-counter (OTC) market

117 Which of the following is least likely to be described as a benefit of derivatives markets?

A Derivatives markets help keep interest rates down

B Derivatives markets supply valuable price information

C Derivatives allow the shifting of risk to those who can most efficiently bear it

D Transactions costs are usually smaller in derivatives markets than for similar trades in the underlying asset

118 Which THREE of the following are advantages of options?

A Provide complete certainty as to the amount to be paid or received

B Simple to understand and cheap to operate

C Provide a means of hedging uncertain transactions

D Guaranteed conformance to hedge accounting requirements

E Provide a guaranteed minimum sum received or maximum sum paid

F Ensure that the cash flows associated with financing the transaction are known in advance

119 A company is looking to take out a loan in 6 months' time for a period of 9 months. LIBOR is currently 3% and the bank has quoted rates of LIBOR + 0.55% on the following forward rates for LIBOR:

7 v 16   3.5 – 3.75

6 v 15   3.45 – 3.7

What is the effective rate that the company will pay?

A 4.30%

B 4.25%

C 4.05%

D 4.00%

120 Company A would like to take out a variable rate loan for a new project. Company B also has a new project but would like to take out a fixed rate loan in order to have certainty over interest payments.

Company A has been quoted a fixed rate of 7% and a variable rate of LIBOR+4%. Company B has been quoted a fixed rate of 6% and a variable rate of LIBOR+2% as it has a higher credit rating than A.

If they enter into a swap arrangement, what effective rate will each end up paying?

A Co A 7%   Co B LIBOR + 2%

B Co A LIBOR + 4%   Co B 6%

C Co A LIBOR + 2%   Co B 7%

D Co A LIBOR + 3.5%   Co B 5.5%

121   Which THREE of the following are advantages of using interest rate swaps?

   A   to manage fixed and floating rate debt profiles without having to change underlying borrowing

   B   to hedge against variations in interest on floating rate debt

   C   to protect the fair value of floating rate debt instruments

   D   to obtain cheaper finance

122   DD Co has a floating rate borrowing, whose interest rate is LIBOR + 1.5%.

   The directors are concerned that interest rates are forecast to rise, so they have approached the bank to discuss the possibility of entering an interest rate swap.

   The bank has quoted a swap rate of 5% against LIBOR.

   If DD Co enters the swap arrangement, what net interest rate will it pay?

   A   LIBOR + 5%

   B   5%

   C   6.5%

   D   3.5%

123   Tither Co needs to deposit GBP 6 million in 12 months' time and is concerned about interest rate risk exposure.

   Which of the following strategies would help Tither Co to manage this risk? Select all that apply.

   A   Sell FRAs

   B   Matching

   C   Buy put options on short term interest rate futures

   D   Buy an interest rate cap

   E   Buy bond futures

   F   Smoothing

124   H (a UK company) must pay USD 2.5 million to an American supplier in nine months' time. The treasurer of H has obtained the following information:

   •   Spot rate is USD 1.2340 – 1.2260 to GBP 1

   •   USD borrowing can be obtained at 4.8% per year and deposits pay 2.6% per year

   •   GBP borrowing can be obtained at 4.0% per year and deposits pay 2.1% per year

   Calculate the cost to H in GBP of a money market hedge, to the nearest GBP 1,000.

   A   2,060,000

   B   2,047,000

   C   2,039,000

   D   1,997,000

125 J (a UK company) expects to receive CAD 1.7 million from a Canadian customer in four months' time. The treasurer of H has obtained the following information:

- Spot rate is CAD 1.7580 – 1.7440 to GBP 1

- CAD borrowing can be obtained at 3.3% per year and deposits pay 1.8% per year

- GBP borrowing can be obtained at 4.0% per year and deposits pay 2.1% per year

Calculate the expected receipt to J in GBP of a money market hedge, to the nearest GBP 1,000.

A   956,000

B   963,000

C   971,000

D   976,000

126 Q (a French company) expects to receive GBP 1.2 million from a UK customer in six months' time. The treasurer of H has obtained the following information:

- Spot rate is EUR 1.1800 – 1.1000 to GBP 1

- EUR borrowing can be obtained at 5.0% per year and deposits pay 2.4% per year

- GBP borrowing can be obtained at 4.0% per year and deposits pay 2.1% per year

Calculate the expected receipt to Q in EUR of a money market hedge, to the nearest EUR 1,000.

A   1,082,000

B   1,300,000

C   1,310,000

D   1,405,000

127 **Assume that today is the 31st March.**

A company is going to deposit $3,500,000 in two months' time for a period of five months. It fears that the current interest rate will fall from its current level of 4%, so it wants to use $500,000 3-month interest rate futures to hedge the position.

Data from the futures market:

March futures price = 95.70

June futures price = 95.40

September futures price = 95.25

Select the THREE answers below that are required to set up a hedge using interest rate futures?

A   Sell futures

B   Buy futures

C   Use March futures

D   Use June futures

E   Use September futures

F   Need 7 contracts

G   Need 11 contracts

H   Need 12 contracts

128 Assume that today is the 20th July.

A company is going to borrow $3,300,000 in two months' time for a period of six months. It fears that the current interest rate will rise from its current level of 6%, so it wants to use $500,000 3-month interest rate futures to hedge the position.

Data from the futures market:

June futures price = 93.80

September futures price = 93.55   ·

Calculate the result of the relevant futures hedge on the assumption that interest rates have risen to 8% and the futures price has moved to 92.13 in two months' time.

A   Net cost $108,925

B   Net cost $110,700

C   Net cost $132,000

D   Net cost $155,075

129 D (a UK company) has made an export sale of USD 450,000. Receipt is due in 60 days.

The current spot rate is GBP1 = USD 1.4820 – 1.4670.

There is a two-month forward at a discount of 2.6 cents – 1.7 cents.

What is the amount of GBP that D will receive using the forward hedge?

A   GBP 298,408

B   GBP 303,234

C   GBP 306,748

D   GBP 310,345

130 E (a UK company) has imported goods at a cost of EUR 285,000. Payment is due in 60 days.

The current spot rate is GBP1 = EUR 1.1200 – 1.0986.

There is a two-month forward quoted at a premium of 1.9 cents – 1.5 cents.

What is the amount of GBP that E will pay using the forward hedge?

A   GBP 250,219

B   GBP 254,464

C   GBP 258,856

D   GBP 263,012

131 It is currently 1st June, and a UK company sells goods to a US company to the value of USD 2.85 million today which is payable in 75 days' time. The current spot rate is USD 1.5800 per GBP 1. A June futures contract is quoted as USD 1.5790. A September futures contract is quoted as USD 1.5200.

Sterling futures are traded in contracts of GBP 62,500. The UK company always buys the minimum number of contracts, being prepared to leave un-hedged any small residual amount.

Select the THREE answers below that are required for the UK company to set up a hedge using futures?

A   Sell futures

B   Buy futures

C   Use June futures

D   Use September futures

E   Need 28 contracts

F   Need 30 contracts

G   Need 45 contracts

132 It is currently 1st February, and a UK company buys goods from a Spanish company to the value of EUR 1 million today which is payable on 22nd June. The current spot rate is EUR 1.1620 per GBP 1. A June futures contract is quoted as EUR 1.1800. A September futures contract is quoted as EUR 1.1870.

Sterling futures are traded in contracts of GBP 62,500. The UK company always rounds the number of contracts to the nearest whole number.

On 22nd June the spot rate is EUR 1.1785 per GBP 1 and the relevant futures price is EUR 1.1865. What will the total gain/loss on the contracts be, if they are closed out on 22nd June?

A   Gain of GBP 5,688

B   Loss of GBP 5,688

C   Gain of GBP 4,826

D   Loss of GBP 4,826

133 It is 1st October and T has identified the need to convert euros into dollars to pay a US supplier USD 5 million on 17th December. The treasurer has decided to use December euro futures contracts to hedge with the following details:

- Contract size EUR 250,000.

- Prices given in USD per EUR (i.e. EUR1 = ...).

- Tick size USD 0.0001 or USD 25 per contract.

T opens a position on 1st October and closes it on 17th December. Spot and relevant futures prices are as follows:

Date	Spot	Futures price
1st October	1.0800	1.1530
17th December	1.1260	1.1340

What is the net cost in euros to T on 17th December?

A   EUR 4,336,513

B   EUR 4,368,783

C   EUR 4,440,497

D   EUR 4,512,211

134 AH, an American based company, has sold goods on credit to a Japanese customer. It has invoiced in Japanese Yen (JPY) for 227 million.

The exchange rate is currently JPY 107.8 to USD 1.

The daily volatility of the exchange rate is 0.62%.

What is the 7-day 96% VAR, to the nearest USD 1,000?

A   USD 60,000

B   USD 25,000

C   USD 23,000

D   USD 13,000

135 M is a company based in South Africa that has just made a large sale to a customer based in Australia invoiced in Australian dollars which is payable in 60 days' time. M is worried that the Australian dollar will depreciate between now and when the invoice is due for payment.

To which risk is M concerned about?

A Translation risk

B Economic risk

C Transaction risk

D Political risk

SYLLABUS SECTION D: BUSINESS VALUATION

136 **Which THREE of the following reasons are often given as reasons for a spin-off?**

A to reduce the risk of a takeover bid for the core entity

B to divest of a less profitable business unit if an acceptable offer is received

C to generate cash in a time of crisis

D to allow investors to identify the true value of a business that was hidden within a large conglomerate

E to give a clearer management structure

137 Asset stripping is a common reason given by entities as why they wish to buy a target company.

What is asset stripping?

A Buying a small percentage of the share capital of the target company

B Purchasing all of the share capital of the target company and also settling the entity's debts

C Buying all the share capital of the business and then selling off the assets

D Purchasing the assets of a target company on a piecemeal basis

138 Mr S and Mrs Q are the managers of Spring Co, an underperforming subsidiary of Season Co. They are in the process of putting together a bid to use a management buyout (MBO) to take control of Spring Co by buying the company from Season Co.

The plan is that the managers themselves will invest 20% of the necessary funds and the other 80% will be provided by a venture capitalist and a bank. Over the next five years, if the MBO goes ahead and is successful, Mr S and Mrs Q plan to increase their stake incrementally by buying out the venture capitalist year by year.

Which THREE of the following reasons could explain why Spring Co might be more successful after the MBO?

A Greater motivation for the managers to succeed

B Better objectives set by managers who understand the business better

C Greater economies of scale

D More flexibility to change without having to wait for parent company approval

E No need to pay dividends to Season Co

139 Venture capitalists often provide finance to help with management buyouts.

Which of the following reasons best explains why management buyouts are generally structured so that the venture capital finance is a mixture of equity and debt?

A   Because the Traditional View of gearing suggests that the optimum financing structure is a mix of debt and equity

B   Because 100% debt finance would be too risky

C   Because 100% equity finance means that the entity forgoes tax relief on debt interest

D   Because the venture capitalist wants some equity finance to provide a high rate of return, but not so much that it takes control of the company

140 **If a company believes that after acquiring another company, it will be in a better position to access low cost debt finance, this would be categorised as:**

A   a synergy of complementary resources

B   an economy of scale

C   an economy of vertical integration

D   bootstrapping

141 Shaw Inc is a software development business and is based in the USA. Luke Co is a service business that writes bespoke computer programs for its clients. It is based in the UK.

Luke Co has made an offer to buy Shaw Inc.

What would this type of acquisition be best described as?

A   Horizontal Integration

B   Portfolio Acquisition

C   Vertical Integration

D   None of the above

142 **What is a reverse takeover?**

A   The buyer pulls out of the purchase of the vendor business at the eleventh hour

B   The acquisition of a larger company by a smaller company

C   Certain assets of an entity are hived off to a new subsidiary company and then this subsidiary is sold off

D   A company sells a small part of its business to selective members of its management team

143 Herra Inc is an engineering business making parts for the car industry. Anders Co is a small family-owned entity that retails car parts for local car mechanics.

Herra has made an offer to buy Anders.

What would this type of acquisition be best described as?

A   Horizontal Integration

B   Portfolio Acquisition

C   Vertical Integration

D   None of the above

144 Many countries have set up regulators (for example the UK has The Competition and Markets Authority (CMA)) to oversee merger and acquisition activity.

What is the main role of such regulators?

A   To ensure that the buyer and seller arrive at a fair price for the vendor business

B   To mediate between the buyer and seller when there is a hostile take-over

C   To protect relevant stakeholders as the combined buyer and seller may wield monopoly power

D   To advise the government on merger and acquisition law

145 Nuruk Inc intends to launch a hostile takeover bid for Penn Co. The companies are direct competitors. The directors of Penn Co have heard rumours that the bid is about to be made, but they don't think that a takeover by Nuruk Inc would be in the best interests of Penn Co's shareholders.

Which of the following defence strategies could be used by Penn Co?

A   Make a counter bid

B   Find a white knight

C   Refer the bid to the competition authorities

D   Change the Articles of Association to require a greater proportion of shareholders (super majority) to vote to accept any bid

146 **Which TWO of the following reasons could be used as a justification for a spin-off?**

A   To raise cash for further investment

B   To eliminate diseconomies of scale

C   To pay excess cash back to shareholders

D   To comply with a legal or regulatory requirement

E   To enable the managers of a business unit to take control of their business

147 King Co is the subject of a rumoured takeover from Queen Co, although no firm offer has yet been made.

Which THREE of the following strategic defence methods could be used by the directors of King Co in this situation?

A   White knight

B   Pacman

C   Appeal to the shareholders to reject any forthcoming offer

D   Poison pill

E   Super majority

148 **Which of the following benefits generated from a merger of two independent entities would NOT be classified as a synergy from operating economies?**

A   an economy of scale

B   bootstrapping

C   an economy of vertical integration

D   complementary resources

149 **Which of the following is the BEST definition of bootstrapping?**

A   an increase in value generated when an entity with a low P/E ratio acquires an entity with a higher P/E ratio

B   an increase in value generated when an entity with a high P/E ratio acquires an entity with a lower P/E ratio

C   the synergy created by merging the activities of two similar sized entities

D   the gains made by a target entity's shareholders during the process of acquisition

150 A listed company, Noon Co, is in negotiations with an unlisted company, Hall Co, regarding a possible takeover of the entire equity capital of the company.

Noon Co's directors have offered to purchase Hall Co's shares at a price that is 20% higher than the price charged when a parcel of 10% of Hall Co's shares was sold last month.

Which of the following reasons is LEAST likely to explain why Noon Co has offered to pay a high price for the Hall Co shares?

A   Noon Co expects there to be significant synergistic gains from the acquisition

B   Noon Co understands that a premium will have to be paid when acquiring a controlling interest

C   Noon Co has used a different method of business valuation from the one used when the 10% parcel of shares was valued

D   Noon Co thinks that some of Hall Co's shareholders (especially the new shareholder who bought the 10% holding recently) may be unwilling to sell unless a significant premium is offered

151 Country T and Country V are separated by sea but linked by a rail tunnel.

They have different currencies (T$ and V$ respectively) but are part of the same Trade Group which promotes free trade between its members and has authority over membership countries in matters relating to competition.

TNL is a public listed company, based in Country T, which owns and operates the rail link between Country T and Country V. Trains that travel through the tunnel carry passengers, cars and other vehicles such as trucks.

There is strong price competition between TNL and two independent ferry companies, TT and VV which are based in Countries T and V respectively. Prices are generally low for travel by ferry since ferries are less convenient as they operate less frequently and have longer journey times than the rail tunnel link. TT has incurred losses in the past two years.

The board of TNL has approached ferry company TT with a view to acquiring it.

The directors of TT are opposed to the bid and have referred the bid to the regional competition authorities of both Country T and the Trade Group.

Which THREE of the following are likely reasons for TNL wanting to acquire TT?

   A   To obtain synergies of vertical integration

   B   To increase market power

   C   To obtain tax relief

   D   To increase market share

   E   Diversification of risk

152 Muller Co is a sportswear manufacturer. It has just made a bid for Biglia Co, a similar company based in a different country.

Both companies are listed on their respective country's stock exchanges and the day the bid was announced, the share prices of both companies rose.

Which of the following is NOT a sensible explanation as to why this happened?

   A   The stock markets are strongly efficient

   B   Investors believe that the takeover will increase their wealth

   C   The market believes that synergy will be generated as a consequence of the takeover

   D   Biglia Co and Muller Co are perceived as being a good strategic fit

153 The competition authorities have been asked to investigate the takeover of Lager Co, a café-bar company, by a larger company Bitter Co.

Which of the following is LEAST likely to be the outcome of the investigation?

   A   The takeover is allowed to proceed, subject to a higher payment being made by Bitter Co to the Lager Co shareholders

   B   The takeover is blocked

   C   The takeover is allowed to proceed

   D   The takeover is allowed to proceed, subject to a limit on the number of retail outlets that the combined entity can own

154 Gina Co is selling off an underperforming, loss making part of its business called JJ Co. Tommy Co has made a bid for JJ Co. The directors of Tommy Co intend merging JJ Co with an existing part of the Tommy Co business and expect the newly merged business unit to be profitable and successful.

Which of the following reasons is LEAST likely to explain why Tommy Co will be able to generate more profits from this business unit than Gina Co could?

   A   Synergies will be generated between Tommy Co and JJ Co

   B   Tommy Co has more experienced managers than Gina Co has

   C   JJ Co has a better strategic fit with Tommy Co than with Gina Co

   D   Tommy Co has a higher cost of capital than Gina Co

155 Country T and Country V are separated by sea but linked by a rail tunnel.

They have different currencies (T$ and V$ respectively) but are part of the same Trade Group which promotes free trade between its members and has authority over membership countries in matters relating to competition.

TNL is a public listed company, based in Country T, which owns and operates the rail link between Country T and Country V. Trains that travel through the tunnel carry passengers, cars and other vehicles such as trucks.

There is strong price competition between TNL and two independent ferry companies, TT and VV which are based in Countries T and V respectively. Prices are generally low for travel by ferry since ferries are less convenient as they operate less frequently and have longer journey times than the rail tunnel link. TT has incurred losses in the past two years.

The board of TNL has approached ferry company TT with a view to acquiring it.

The directors of TT are opposed to the bid and have referred the bid to the regional competition authorities of both Country T and the Trade Group.

Which of the following is LEAST likely to be of concern to the competition authorities?

   A   TNL and TT combined might be able to start a price war to force VV out of business

   B   TT's directors are opposed to the bid

   C   Prices for customers might rise after the takeover

   D   The takeover might not be in the public interest

156 An all equity company is just about to pay a dividend of $0.60 per share. The company confidently expects the dividend to grow at 10% a year. The company has estimated its cost of capital to be 13%.

What would you expect the current quoted share price to be?

   A $22.00

   B $22.60

   C $20.00

   D $20.60

157   Alpha Co reported a profit before interest and tax of $3.5 million in its most recent accounts. The company is mainly equity financed, but has a $2 million bank borrowing on which it pays 10% per year in interest. The rate of corporate income tax is 25%.

Assuming that Alpha Co's P/E ratio is 8, what is the value of the company's equity?

A $28.0 million

B $26.0 million

C $19.8 million

D $17.8 million

158   GGG Co is intending to take over FFF Co.

GGG Co has a P/E ratio of 10 and post-tax earnings of $5m, and FFF Co has a P/E ratio of 8 and post-tax earnings of $3m.

GGG's directors estimate that if they were to acquire FFF there would be annual synergies of $0.5m for the new combined company. Additionally they estimate that the P/E ratio of the new company would be 9.5.

On the basis of these estimates, what is the maximum that GGG should pay for the entire share capital of FFF?

A $24.00 million

B $30.75 million

C $33.25 million

D $80.75 million

159   The most recent financial statements for Nye Co show the following:

	$000
Interest	210
Investment in Non-Current Assets	378
Dividends	134
Operating Profit	879
Investment in Working Capital	143
Depreciation	167

The company pays tax on company profits at the rate of 22%.

What is Nye Co's free cash flow to equity (to the nearest $000)?

A $68,000

B $168,000

C $332,000

D $335,000

160 **Which of the following correctly describes the discounted cash flow method that can be used to value an entity's equity?**

    A   Deduct interest and dividends in arriving at the forecast cash flows and then discount the latter at the cost of equity

    B   Discount the forecast free cash flows to equity at the entity's WACC and then deduct the market value of the entity's debt

    C   Forecast the cash flows, without deducting taxation, and discount these at the entity's WACC

    D   Deduct interest but not dividends in arriving at the forecast cash flows and then discount the latter at the cost of equity

161 **Win Co wishes to ascertain the value of its equity. It has prepared the following schedule of forecast post-tax cash flows before financing charges:**

$m	Year 1	Year 2	Year 3	Year 4
	283	291	298	305

The forecast cash flows are expected to grow at rate of 3% per annum after year 4 into perpetuity. Win Co has a cost of equity of 15% and a WACC of 12%. The entity's debt is believed to be worth 30% of the total value of the entity.

What is the value of Win Co's equity?

    A $891m

    B $2,178m

    C $2,536m

    D $3,111m

162 Eden Inc has recently published its latest accounts showing profit after tax of $23.12m, after deducting interest of $4.89m. Tax allowable depreciation was $4.55m and the company expects profits to grow at 5% per annum indefinitely.

The company policy is to maintain its asset base by reinvesting cash to a value equal to the tax allowable depreciation. Eden has estimated its cost of equity at 12%, which is included in the company WACC of 10%

Assuming that profit after tax is the equivalent to cash flows, what is the value of the equity capital?

    A $346.80m

    B $485.52m

    C $588.21m

    D $683.76m

163 Tanu Inc has 1 million $0.50 par value shares in issue. It generated free cash flow to equity of $1.5 million last year and expects this figure to grow by 4% per annum in the future.

Tanu Inc has a cost of equity of 14% and a WACC of 10%. It has $500,000 of bonds in issue, trading at $80 per $100.

What is the estimated value of a Tanu Inc share?

A $7.80

B $12.80

C $15.60

D $25.60

164 Company A and Company B operate in the same industry, but have different price earnings (P/E) ratios as follows:

	P/E ratio
Company A	8
Company B	15

Which of the following is the most probable explanation of the difference in the P/E ratios between the two companies?

A   Company B has a greater profit this year than Company A

B   Company B is higher risk than Company A

C   Company B has higher expected growth than Company A

D   Company B has higher gearing than Company A

165 A company has 70,000 issued shares at 50c per share which are currently trading for 204c.

The company paid $6,000 in dividends to ordinary shareholders and $2,000 to preference shareholders. Profit after taxation was $17,000 and $10,000 was paid in taxation.

What is the Price Earnings (P/E) ratio of the company?

A   5.3

B   8.4

C   9.5

D   15.8

166 **A high P/E ratio is usually seen as an indication that:**

A   The company's earnings are poor

B   The company is likely to grow

C   The share is over priced

D   The dividend is excessive

167 The published data for Sounders Inc shows:

Earnings per share	20 cents
Dividend cover	4
Dividend yield	2%

What is the current price of Sounders Inc's ordinary shares?

A   25 cents

B   80 cents

C   160 cents

D   250 cents

[Handwritten: 4 × 2 = 8% ; 100/8 = 12.5 ; 20 × 12.5 = 250]

168 The following data is available for Pop Inc:

P/E ratio: 10

Dividend cover: 4 times

Share capital: $2 million in 25c shares

The dividend is 2c per share

What is the total market price of Pop Inc?

A $1.6 million

B $6.4 million

C $8 million

D $64 million

169 Ayai is a company listed on its local stock exchange. An extract from the company's latest accounts shows:

	$000
25 cents ordinary share capital	500
Share premium	1,050
$1 preference shares	3,200
Income reserves	2,135
6.25% bonds	2,300

The ordinary shares are trading at $2.30 and the preference shares are not traded. The bonds are currently priced at $96 per block of $100.

What is the current equity market capitalisation ($000)?

A $3,685

B $4,400

C $4,600

D $9,185

170 Jenduri is a private company that is considering listing its shares for the first time on a local stock exchange via an initial public offering (IPO). They intend to list 30% of their 4 million shares on to the market.

The company advisors have prepared the following schedule of equity valuations per share:

	$
Nominal value	0.50
Net assets – book value	2.34
Net assets – net realisable value	1.72
Dividend valuation model	3.35

What is the most appropriate valuation for the IPO?

A $0.50

B $1.72

C $2.34

D $3.35

171 Sari is a family owned company that manufactures parts to the motor industry. The entity has been struggling in recent years and the owners are now considering their options.

Extracts from the latest accounts show the book value of their assets to be worth:

	$m
Land and buildings	4.10
Plant and machinery	1.30
Inventory	0.85
Trade receivables	0.45

The company has trade payables standing at $0.66m and the bank overdraft is now at $2.15m. The non-current assets would only be worth 42% of the book values if sold immediately. Similarly, the inventory would realise $0.32m if disposed of today. A factoring company has valued the trade receivables at 72% of the book value.

The net cash available to distribute to the shareholders if the business did NOT continue as a going concern is:

$ [   ] (INSERT CORRECT FIGURE IN THE BOX)

172 Zudun Co's equity is currently valued at $598m. Their last reported profit after tax was $52m. ETA Co is a family owned business that operates in the same industry as Zudun Co. ETA's board of directors is considering either a trade sale or a listing via an IPO.

Financial data relating to ETA Co:

Issued ordinary share capital ($1 shares)	3m
Profit after tax	$11.12m
Recently paid dividends	$3.34m
Estimated cost of equity	11%

ETA Co has maintained its current dividend pay-out ratio for the last 5 years.

Complete the following schedule relating to ETA Co:

EPS	$xx.xx
Value per share using dividend valuation model	$xx.xx
Value per share using the P/E model	$xx.xx

173 Company X is hoping to sell 100% of its 1m shares. Its current operating profit is $400,000, its profit after tax is $259,000 and a suitable PE ratio is 14.

What is the value per share for Company X?

A $2.59

B $3.63

C $3.82

D $5.60

174 The following data applies to Abbott Co:

Current P/E ratio = 10

Latest dividends = $2m

Dividend cover = 5

What is the market value of Abbott Co based on a P/E valuation?

A $80m

B $95m

C $100m

D $200m

175 Clare Co is looking to value 100% of its equity.

It currently has a profit after tax of $1.5 million, but this includes an element of profit from the sale of land of $0.325 million. A suitable P/E ratio is 8.

What is the value of Clare Co using a P/E ratio method?

A $9.4 million

B $12 million

C $15.3 million

D $18.7 million

176 The directors of Veena Co, an unlisted entity, want to value the entity's shares using the P/E method.

The entity recently reported a profit after tax of $800,000 – which the directors think is sustainable for the future.

They have found a similar company that is listed that has a P/E ratio of 10. From a full review it is thought that Veena Co is worth about 25% less than the listed company.

What is the value of Veena Co, using the P/E method?

A $4.3 million

B $6 million

C $8 million

D $10.4 million

177 Company A is owned by its three directors and they want to sell the business.

The current profit after tax is $500,000. At the moment the directors are only paid small salaries as they take most of their returns in the form of dividends.

Once the company is sold, the cost of directors' salaries in Company A will need to be increased by $40,000 in total to attract sufficiently high quality new directors.

A suitable P/E ratio is 5 and the tax rate is 30%.

What is the value of Company A, using a P/E valuation?

A $1,800,000

B $2,360,000

C $2,500,000

D $2,832,000

178 After months of planning, Thierry Co released news to the market of its expansion strategy.

Prior to the release, Thierry had a market capitalisation of $42.6 million, an authorised share capital of $1 million and an issued share capital of $500,000 (made up of 50 cent shares).

The expansion strategy is expected to generate an NPV of $5 million.

Assuming strong form market efficiency, what will be the effect on Thierry's share price?

A   Increase by $10

B   Increase by $5

C   No change

D   Increase by $20

179 Miss Coates has been left $20,000 which she plans to invest on the Stock Exchange in order to have a source of capital should she decide to start her own business in a few years' time. A friend of hers who works in the City of London has told her that the London Stock Exchange shows strong form market efficiency.

If this is the case, which of the following investment strategies should Miss Coates follow?

A   Study the company reports in the press and try to spot under-valued shares in which to invest

B   Invest in two or three blue chip companies and hold the shares for as long as possible

C   Build up a good spread of shares in different industry sectors

D   Study the company reports in the press and try to spot strongly growing companies in which to invest

180 Share prices quoted on a stock exchange are observed to move before information about the company's plans becomes publicly available.

Which of the following best describes this form of market efficiency?

A   Weak form

B   Strong form

C   Semi-strong form

D   Not efficient at all

181 **Match the following descriptions with the types of market efficiency.**

Weak form	Extrapolating past share price movements would allow a trader to beat the market.
Strong form	Accurate analysis of public information should allow a trader to beat the market.
No efficiency	All information in a market is accounted for in the share price.
Semi strong efficiency	Traders can only beat the market using insider information.

182 **What is the validity of the following statements?**

1   The existence of projects with positive expected net present values supports the idea that the stock market is strong-form efficient.

2   The existence of information content in dividends supports the idea that the stock market is strong-form efficient.

	Statement 1	Statement 2
A	True	True
B	True	False
C	False	True
D	False	False

183 Asad Co is trying to find the value of its intangible assets using the Calculated Intangible Value (CIV) method. Relevant data is:

Tangible assets	$1.268m
WACC	11%
Ke	14%
Profit before tax	$0.453m
Industry return on tangible assets	15%
Tax Rate	30%

What is the value of Asad Co's intangible assets?

A $1.672m

B $1.314m

C $1.210m

D $0.951m

184 Food2go is a supermarket with a current debt to equity ratio of 30:70 based on market values and it has a current equity beta of 0.8. To expand business it plans to take over an unlisted petrol station company, Petrol King Co, which has an estimated debt to equity ratio of 40:60.

To value Petrol King Co, Food2go intends to use the discounted cash flow approach, so it needs to calculate a suitable cost of equity as a prelude to calculating a weighted average cost of capital (WACC) that can be used for discounting.

A listed petrol station company has an equity beta of 1.8 with a debt to equity ratio of 50:50

The expected return on the market portfolio is 8% and the current return on a risk free investment is 5%. The tax rate is 30%

What cost of equity should be used as part of the WACC for discounting the Petrol King Co cash flows?

A   9.65%

B   9.50%

C   12.00%

D   5.70%

185 A portfolio is equally invested in company A, with an expected return of 6%, company B, with an expected return of 10%, and a risk-free asset with a return of 5%.

The expected return on the portfolio is:

A   6.3%

B   7.0%

C   7.4%

D   8.0%

De gear
re gear

186 Chambers has a debt : equity ratio of 1:2 by market values and an equity beta of 0.9. Debt is assumed to be risk free and has a pre-tax cost of 2% per annum. The expected return on the market portfolio is 8% and corporation tax is 30%.

Chambers wishes to undertake an APV approach for investment appraisal.

What is the ungeared cost of equity for Chambers to use in such an evaluation?

A   6.00%

B   7.40%

C   9.20%

D   9.29%

187 Clyne has a debt : equity ratio of 1:2 by market values and an asset beta of 0.9. Debt is assumed to be risk free and has a pre-tax cost of 2% per annum. The market risk premium is 8% and corporation tax is 30%.

What is Clyne's geared cost of equity?

A   7.40%

B   9.20%

C   9.29%

D   11.72%

188 Fonte has a debt : equity ratio of 1:2 by market values and an equity beta of 0.9. Debt is assumed to be risk free and has a pre-tax cost of 2% per annum. The market risk premium is 8% and corporation tax is 30%.

What is Fonte's geared cost of equity?

A   7.40%

B   9.20%

C   9.29%

D   11.72%

189 Lovren has a debt : equity ratio of 1:2 by market values and an asset beta of 0.9. Debt is assumed to be risk free and has a pre-tax cost of 2% per annum. The expected return on the market portfolio is 8% and corporation tax is 30%.

What is Lovren's geared cost of equity?

A   7.40%

B   9.20%

C   9.29%

D   11.72%

190 Shaw has a debt : equity ratio of 1:2 by market values and an equity beta of 0.9. Debt is assumed to be risk free and has a pre-tax cost of 2% per annum. The expected return on the market portfolio is 8% and corporation tax is 30%.

What is Shaw's geared cost of equity?

A   7.40%

B   9.20%

C   9.29%

D   11.72%

191 You have been asked to calculate the equity beta factor for SIX Co.

Introductory data:

APPLE Co is a listed company in the same industry as SIX Co. It has an equity beta of 1.45.

Gearing levels – (debt/equity) by market value:

SIX Co   45/55

APPLE Co   30/70

Tax rate is 25%. The beta of debt is 0.10.

Which one of the following shows the correct formula for REGEARING the proxy company's ASSET beta (which would be the second step in trying to calculate an equity beta for SIX Co):

A $\beta_g = 1.25 + \left[(1.25 - 0.10) \left(\dfrac{30(1 - 0.25)}{70} \right) \right]$

B $\beta_g = 1.12 + \left[(1.12 - 0.10) \left(\dfrac{30(1 - 0.25)}{70} \right) \right]$

C $\beta_g = 1.12 + \left[(1.12 - 0.10) \left(\dfrac{45(1 - 0.25)}{55} \right) \right]$

D $\beta_g = 1.25 + \left[(1.25 - 0.10) \left(\dfrac{45(1 - 0.25)}{55} \right) \right]$

192 Ocatvio Co is preparing a valuation of Tarte Co, an unlisted company. Tarte Co has an estimated debt to equity ratio of 20% : 80%.

As part of the calculation of a suitable weighted average cost of capital, Octavio Co needs to identify a suitable equity beta for Tarte Co.

The following information has been presented by Octavio Co's Financial Controller, based on three other companies that share the same business risk as Tarte Co, but have different capital structures.

Co A   Equity beta = 1.6   Debt to equity ratio 40:60

Co B   Equity beta = 1.2   Debt to equity ratio 10:90

Co C   Equity beta = 1.8   Debt to equity ratio 50:50

Which of the following is the best estimate of the correct equity beta for Tarte Co?

A   1.0

B   1.4

C   1.7

D   2.0

193 Turtle Power Co is an unlisted company. Its directors are preparing a valuation of the company that will be used in negotiations with a potential purchaser. Hence they need to compute a suitable weighted average cost of capital.

The entity currently has an estimated debt to equity ratio of 15:85. Its debt is approximately risk free and has a pre-tax cost of 4%.

A similar quoted company to Turtle Power Co has an equity beta of 1.2, and a debt to equity ratio of 30:70.

The expected return on the market portfolio is 10% and the tax rate is 30%.

What is the weighted average cost of capital of Turtle Power Co?

A   9.1%

B   9.3%

C   9.9%

D   10.1%

194 Forrest Co has a debt to equity ratio of 30:70 and has an equity beta of 1.4. The tax rate is 30%.

The current return on a risk free asset is 5% and the average market risk premium is 7%.

What is Forrest Co's ungeared cost of equity?

A   5.9%

B   12.6%

C   14.1%

D   20.5%

195 Exercise Co is attempting to derive its cost of equity, based on the following proxy company information: a similar company in the same industry has an equity beta of 1.6 with a debt to equity ratio of 20:80.

Exercise Co has an estimated debt to equity ratio of 30:70.

The expected return on the market portfolio is 8% and the current return on a risk free investment is 4%. The tax rate is 30%

What is Exercise Co's cost of equity?

A 15.0%

B 9.8%

C 11.1%

D 27.6%

196 QPR is a listed company which is seeking to sell WBA, one of its business units, in a management buyout. A selling price of $100 million has been agreed. It is anticipated that the date of the disposal will be 1 January 20X5.

The managers of WBA have been in discussions with a bank and a venture capitalist regarding the financing for the MBO. The financing proposal is:

	$m
Managers – equity	25
VC – equity	15
VC – debt	40
Bank loan	20
	___
Total	100
	___

The venture capitalist expects a return on the equity portion of its investment of at least 20% a year on a compound basis over the first 3 years of the MBO.

What is the minimum total equity value of WBA on 31 December 20X8 required in order to satisfy the venture capitalist's expected return?

A $69.12 million

B $25.92 million

C $18.00 million

D $48.00 million

197 Willis incorporated a new company five years ago. The company has grown quickly and is now large enough to be listed on the stock exchange. Willis owns 100% of the share capital in the company and wishes to realise the full value of his investment.

Which THREE of the following exit strategies could Willis consider?

A   Rights issue of shares

B   Spin off

C   Management buy-out

D   Initial public offering (IPO)

E   Private equity buy-in

198 Company A wishes to acquire company B and is considering how best to structure the consideration. Both companies are of a similar size.

A currently has gearing (D/D+E) of 40%. A's shareholders do not wish to subscribe additional funds at this time.

Structuring the bid offer as a cash offer funded by debt rather than a share exchange is MOST likely to have the effect of:

A   Diluting A shareholders' control

B   Increasing A shareholders' earnings per share

C   Lowering A's gearing (D/D+E)

D   Enabling B's shareholders to participate in future growth in A

199 Two all-equity financed companies, Spain Co and France Co, have identical business risks. Spain Co is valued at $30 million and France Co at $10 million.

The two companies merge via a share exchange which results in Spain Co shareholders holding 75% of the shares of the new merged company.

As a result of synergy, surplus assets of $6 million are sold immediately without affecting the future profitability of the merged company. Half of the proceeds of the disposal are invested in a project with a net present value of $2 million.

What will be the gains to the shareholders of France Co?

A $6.00 million

B $3.75 million

C $1.25 million

D $2.00 million

200 GGG Co takes over FFF Co and pays a price that represents a higher P/E valuation than the current P/E of GGG Co.

GGG Co has some debt in its capital structure, and the purchase consideration is paid by issuing new GGG Co shares. There is no synergy arising from the takeover.

Which of the following would NOT be a likely consequence of this takeover?

A   a reduction in gearing for GGG Co

B   an increase in the share price after the takeover

C   a reduction in the proportionate stake in the company of existing GGG Co shareholders

D   a dilution of earnings of GGG Co

201 Stone Co is hoping to make a successful takeover offer for Angel Co.

Stone Co is a large listed company, with a wide range of both institutional and private shareholders.

It has relatively low cash reserves and a gearing ratio of 40% that is higher than most similar companies in its industry.

Which TWO of the following would be feasible ways of structuring an offer for Angel Co?

A   Cash offer, funded by borrowings

B   Share for share exchange

C   Cash offer, funded from existing cash resources

D   Cash offer, funded by a rights issue

E   Debt for share exchange

202 SS has proposed a 1-for-3 share for share exchange with the shareholders of TT, so that SS can acquire TT.

The two companies operate in the same industry and it is estimated that synergy with a present value of $2 million will be generated by the combination.

Currently, SS has 12 million shares in issue, trading at $6.76, and TT has 3 million shares in issue trading at $1.97.

What is the expected share price in the combined company after the takeover?

A $6.85

B $6.76

C $5.91

D $3.17

203 Udika Co has agreed buy all the share capital of Tito Co. The board of directors of Udika Co believes that the post-acquisition value of their business including Tito can be computed using the 'bootstrapping' method.

This can be found by:

A   Combining the pre-acquisition market capitalisation of each company

B   Adding together the current post tax earnings of each company and multiplying this by the price earnings ratio of Tito

C   Adding together the current post tax earnings of each company and multiplying this by the price earnings ratio of Udika

D   Forecasting the future cash flows of the combined entities and discounting these at Udika's WACC

204   Which of the following best describes an earn-out?

A   an arrangement where the owners/managers selling an entity receive a portion of their consideration linked to the financial performance of the business

B   a situation where an entity is valued using the price-earnings ratio

C   a method of splitting the profits of an entity between its various financial stakeholders

D   a situation where an entity generates more than a quarter of its earnings from activities different from its main line of business

205 Oban Co has agreed the purchase of all of the share capital of Reeves Inc. Relevant financial details are:

Boot Strapping — 20

Reeves EPS	$0.34
Oban profit after tax	$25.2m
Oban – number of issued shares	126m
Oban – current share price	$4.00
Reeves – current share price	$4.25
Reeves – number of shares in issue	20m

If Oban can maintain its current P/E ratio, what is the value of the synergy gained from acquiring Reeves?

A $51m

B $85m

C $145m

D $563m

206 Fitness Co is an unlisted company, which was incorporated five years ago and is still 90% owned by its founding family.

The managers are planning to embark upon a period of expansion by acquisition, but the company has very little cash. Therefore, a share for share exchange is being considered in order for Fitness Co to acquire Dumbell Co, a similar sized company in the same industry whose shareholders are keen to realise cash from their investment.

Which of the following problems is LEAST likely to be an issue in this situation?

    A   Fitness Co's founding family will suffer a significant dilution in control

    B   Dumbell Co's shareholders will find it difficult to evaluate the bid given that Fitness Co is unlisted

    C   Fitness Co has very little cash, so won't be able to afford to take over Dumbell Co

    D   Dumbell Co's shareholders will not receive the cash that they require in a share for share exchange

207 MMM is intending to make a bid for JJJ.

MMM has 30 million shares in issue and a current share price of $6.90 before any public announcement of the planned takeover.

JJJ has 5 million shares in issue and a current share price of $12.84.

The directors of MMM are considering making a share based bid of 2 MMM shares for each JJJ share. Overall estimated synergistic benefits of the acquisition are estimated to be in the order of $8 million.

What is the likely gain in wealth for the MMM shareholders if the bid is accepted?

    A $2.40 million

    B $5.60 million

    C $6.98 million

    D $8.00 million

208 AB has recently approached the shareholders of YZ with a bid of 5 new shares in AB for every 6 YZ shares. There is a cash alternative of 345 cents per share.

Following the announcement of the bid, the market price of AB shares fell 10% while the price of YZ shares rose 14%.

Enter the correct word from the choices given:

The market believes that the shareholders of _____ **(AB/YZ)** will receive most of the benefit from this acquisition.

This could be because the value of the offer is too _____ **(high/low).**

209 **Enter the correct word from the choices given, to create two statements that apply to a share for share exchange:**

Compared to a cash offer, a share for share exchange is _____ **(more/less)** likely to create a liability to capital gains tax.

A share for share exchange will benefit the target company's shareholders more than a cash offer if the combined entity performs _____ **(well/badly)** after the acquisition.

210 The directors of Q have approached the directors of Z with a view to making a takeover bid for Z, an owner-managed business.

The directors of Q want to retain the board of directors of Z, who have vital knowledge of the specialist manufacturing techniques required to manufacture the product range of Z.

The directors of Z have been initially quite positive about the bid.

Which of the following types of offer would be MOST suitable in these circumstances?

A   Cash offer

B   Share for share exchange

C   Earnout

D   Debt for share exchange

211 LP and MQ are two listed companies.

LP made an opening bid one week ago of 2 LP shares for 1 MQ share, but MQ's shareholders have rejected the bid.

	LP	MQ
Share price as at today (20 May 20X9)	$3.05	$6.80
Share price one month ago	$3.10	$6.10
Shares in issue (million)	480	130

Which of the following bids would the MQ shareholders be MOST likely to accept?

A   1.97 LP shares for 1 MQ share

B   2.23 LP shares for 1 MQ share

C   2.5 LP shares for 1 MQ share

D   3 LP shares for 1 MQ share

212 Astor Co is planning to acquire Baker Co.

Astor Co currently has post tax earnings of $23.5 million and a P/E ratio of 9. Baker Co currently has post tax earnings of $9.5 million and a P/E ratio of 7.

What is the value of the synergy that will be generated by the combination of Astor Co and Baker Co, assuming that the market uses bootstrapping to calculate the value of the combined entity?

A   Nil

B $19.0 million

C $66.5 million

D $278.0 million

213 Glenderaterra Co and Mungrisdale Co are planning to merge using a share for share exchange. Glenderaterra Co has offered one of its shares for every three shares in Mungrisdale Co.

The directors expect that $10 million of synergy will be generated by combining the two entities.

Current market information shows:

	Glenderaterra	Mungrisdale
Share price	$3.88	$1.10
Shares in issue (million)	50	12

What share of the synergy gain will accrue to the shareholders of Mungrisdale?

A   None

B   29%

C   71%

D   91%

214 Orc Co is considering a takeover bid for Sauron Co.

In which of the following circumstances is a debt for share exchange likely to be MOST suitable?

A   Sauron Co's shareholders are keen to realise cash for their investment

B   Orc Co has a gearing level higher than the average for companies in its industry

C   Sauron Co's shareholders want to maintain an interest in the combined company, but the Orc Co shareholders do not want to suffer a dilution of control

D   Sauron Co is a small company, and its shareholders are the same people as its lenders

215 MMM is intending to make a bid for JJJ.

MMM has 30 million shares in issue and a current share price of $6.90 before any public announcement of the planned takeover.

JJJ has 5 million shares in issue and a current share price of $12.84.

The directors of MMM are considering making a cash offer of $13.50 per JJJ share. Overall estimated synergistic benefits of the acquisition are estimated to be in the order of $8 million.

What is the likely change in wealth for the MMM shareholders if the bid is accepted?

A   Loss of $59.50 million

B   No change

C   Gain of $4.70 million

D   Gain of $8.00 million

216 Big has agreed to acquire Small.

Big currently has 11 million shares in issue and a current share price of $5 before any public announcement of the planned takeover.

Small has 8 million shares in issue and a current share price of $2.75.

It is estimated that synergies with a total value of $7.5m will be generated.

The directors of Big are planning making a 1 for 2 share for share exchange (so Small's shareholders would receive 1 share in Big for every 2 shares they currently own in Small)

What is the likely change in wealth for the Small shareholders if the bid is accepted?

A   Decrease of 0.7%

B   No change

C   Increase of 2.3%

D   Increase of 12.6%

217 Frodo Co is planning a takeover of Sam Co. Frodo has 5m shares trading at $4.93 each and had a latest profit after tax (PAT) of $1.45m. Sam has 7m shares trading at $3.10 each and a latest PAT of $1.55m.

If Frodo plans to use bootstrapping to value the acquisition, what is the total value of the expected synergies?

A $4.7m

B $5.8m

C $17.0m

D $21.7m

218 Zeynab wishes to buy a rival company and is trying to calculate a suitable cost of equity to use in the valuation. The target company is unquoted but is estimated to have a gearing ratio (debt to equity) of 2:5. The industry average gearing (debt / debt + equity) is 25% and the average equity beta is 1.14. Debt is assumed to be risk free and has a pre-tax cost of 3% per annum. Tax is 30%

What is a suitable equity beta that Zeynab could use to help value the target company?

A   0.92

B   1.05

C   1.14

D   1.18

219 Maya Co is an unquoted company, which is 85% owned by the Maya family. Employees of the company own all the remaining shares.

Maya is looking to raise money to grow the business by acquisition. The Maya family are unwilling to give up control and wish the current high level of dividends to continue. Gearing levels are significantly below average industry levels.

Which of the following is MOST likely to be a suitable way of raising finance in this situation?

A   Bank loan

B   Bond issue

C   Retained earnings

D   IPO

220 Luka is trying to find the value of its intangible assets using the Calculated Intangible Value (CIV) method. The latest financial statements showed profit before tax (PBT) of $2.77m. Tangible assets totalled $9m and the industry average return on tangible assets is 18%. Luka has a WACC of 15% and tax is 30%.

What is the total value of Luka?

A $5.4m

B $12.4m

C $14.4m

D $16.7m

Section 2

ANSWERS TO OBJECTIVE TEST QUESTIONS

SYLLABUS SECTION A: FINANCIAL POLICY DECISIONS

1 A

Although the over-riding objective of every listed company is to maximise shareholder wealth, the specific financial objectives listed in a company's annual report would not normally make reference to this.

The gearing objective is too vague (B) because gearing can be measured in several different ways (e.g. debt to equity or debt to (debt + equity) and at book value or at market value).

The expansion objective should contain numbers so that its achievement can be measured (C) – all objectives should be measurable.

The dividend growth objective should be linked to company performance (D) or there is a danger that earnings growth might not keep up with dividend growth, causing financial difficulties.

2 A, D

Both for-profit and not-for-profit entities aim to satisfy a wide range of stakeholders (B).

Not-for-profit entities don't have profit oriented objectives but they may well have financial objectives (C).

3 A

Current post-tax profit is [5m – (3m × 15%)](1 – 0.20) = $3.64 million, so target post-tax profit (up 10%) is $4.004 million.

Hence pre-tax profit target is (4.004 × 100/80 =) $5.005 million, and profit before interest and tax needs to be $5.005m + ($3m × 15%) = $5.455 million

4 A

Interest cover is PBIT/Interest = 75,000/(7% × $400,000) = 2.678

In order for the interest cover to be 3, the PBIT needs to be 3 × (7% × $400,000) = $84,000

This is an increase of 12% over the current PBIT of $75,000.

5   D

Revised statement of profit or loss, reflecting a 10% increase in selling prices and a tax rate of 28%.

	$ million
Revenue (23.6m × 1.10)	26.0
Operating costs	(8.6)
Operating profit	17.4
Interest (10% on bank borrowings)	(3.4)
Profit before tax	14.0
Tax (28%)	(3.9)
Earnings	10.1

This is an increase of 16.1% over the previous figure of $8.7 million.

6   B

Interest cover is PBIT/Interest.

Interest is (coupon rate applied to nominal value) 8% × $1.5 million = $120,000.

If earnings (profit after tax) are $800,000, then PBIT is found by adding back tax and interest.

Therefore, PBIT = (800,000 × 100/80) + 120,000 = $1,120,000

Interest cover is then 1,120,000/120,000 = 9.3 times.

7   B

Revised statement of profit or loss, reflecting a 12% interest rate and a tax rate of 21%.

	$ million
Revenue	23.6
Operating costs	(8.6)
Operating profit	15.0
Interest (12%, so 3.4m × 12/10)	(4.1)
Profit before tax	10.9
Tax (21%)	(2.3)
Earnings	8.6

This is a decrease of approximately 1% from the previous figure of $8.7 million.

8 The answer is **$9.75 million**

	$ million
Sales (up 6%)	53
Cost of sales	23
Gross profit	30
Other operating costs	7
Operating profit	23
Financing costs	10
	13
Tax (now 25%)	(3.25)
Earnings	9.75

9 The answer is **$6.98 million**

Current year profit after tax (PAT)

= [$10m − (9% × $15m)] × (1 − 0.20) = $6.92 million

Next year's PAT is expected to be:

= [($10m × 1.05) − (9% × $15m) − ($6m × 7%)] × (1-0.20)

= $6.98 million

10 **B**

The GBP 60 million revenue in the recent year is made up of GBP 30 million and USD 45 million (i.e. GBP 30 million when converted into GBP at the current exchange rate of 1 GBP = 1.50 USD). If the GBP strengthens by 10% against the USD, the exchange rate will become 1.50 × 1.10 = 1.65 USD to 1 GBP. Therefore, assuming all else is equal, the statement of profit or loss will become:

	GBP million
Revenue (30m + (45m/1.65))	57.3
Operating costs	(35)
Operating profit	22.3
Interest	(10)
Profit before tax	12.3
Tax (20%)	(2.5)
Earnings	9.8

11   A

When the US dollar depreciates, the opposing currency appreciates (inverse relationship). The depreciation of the dollar means that foreign goods become more expensive and import prices will increase. Conversely, as the value of the dollar decreases, US goods become cheaper to foreign customers and US export prices will decrease.

12   C

$[^5 \sqrt{((2.9/2.2)}] - 1 = 5.7\%$

13   D

$[^4 \sqrt{((0.28/0.20)}] - 1 = 8.8\%$

14   A

Dividend per share has grown from $12 (120/10) to $13.08 (170/13).

Therefore the annual growth in dividend per share is:

$[^4 \sqrt{((13.08/12)}] - 1 = 2.2\%$

15   A

GRI 101 – Foundation lays out the Reporting Principles for report content and report quality. These give guidance on which topics should be deemed material and what information should be disclosed.

16   A, B, E

C is an objective of sustainability reporting.

D is irrelevant – investors are more interested in the quality, not the quantity, of information available.

17   A, D, E

The other two are Principles for Defining Report Quality according to the GRI.

18   B

In exceptional cases, if it is not possible to disclose certain required information, the report should clearly identify the information that has been omitted, and explain the reasons why the information has been omitted.

19   B

Social and relationship capitals include intangibles associated with the brand and reputation that an organisation has developed.

20   D

21   A, C, F

(C) and (F) are simply the wrong way round i.e. Risks and opportunities are really a content element and Consistency and comparability is a guiding principle.

(A) should not appear in an Integrated Report. However it would appear as a disclosure in a sustainability report prepared using the GRI Guidelines.

22   B, D

Paying a large dividend to shareholders (A) will make no difference to the wealth of shareholders. Raising new equity finance (C) in an all-equity financed entity will not affect the cost of capital and will not affect shareholder wealth (unless the finance raised is invested in a positive NPV project).

A positive NPV project increases shareholder wealth (B).

If an all-equity financed company raises debt finance (D) its cost of capital will fall, giving an increase in the NPVs generated from projects and hence an increase in shareholder wealth.

23   A, C, D

A single supplier will be seen as a risky characteristic by the bank.

A clear order book for a manufacturing company is again potentially risky. Unless new orders are received, Napoli Co might see a drop in income and therefore might struggle to service the bank borrowing.

24   Thursday Co will probably find it **easier** to raise debt finance than Cass Co.

The rate of interest on borrowings is likely to be **lower** for Thursday Co than Cass Co.

25   Holding **too little** cash will potentially leave the entity subject to liquidity problems and possible liquidation.

Holding **too much** cash has an opportunity cost (lost interest on deposits, or returns on attractive investments).

Holding **too much** cash leaves an entity vulnerable to a takeover bid.

26   D

The thin capitalisation rules aim to prevent companies from getting excessive tax relief on interest.

27 **B**

	With 100% equity	With 60% equity
EBIT	$300,000	$300,000
Interest expense	$0	$24,000
		($480,000 @ 5%)
Profit before tax	$300,000	$276,000
Tax @ 30%	$90,000	$82,800
Net profit	$210,000	$193,200
Equity	$1,200,000	$720,000
ROE = Net profit/Equity	17.5%	26.8%

28 **D**

Dividend growth:

From $0.55m to $0.70m amounts to approximately 27.3% growth in total

(= [0.70/0.55] − 1).

Over three years, the annual growth is found by taking $[\sqrt[3]{}\ 1.273] − 1 = 8.4\%$, so above the target of 7% − objective achieved

Gearing:

Debt value is $105 × 10,000 = $1.05 million

Equity value is 2 million × $1.24 = $2.48 million

So [debt/(debt + equity)] = [1.05/(1.05 + 2.48)] = 29.7%, so below the target of 30% − objective achieved

29 **B**

Interest cover will be

[25m/(6% × 60m) + (5% × 40m)] = 4.46, which is above the level set by the covenant so the covenant is not breached.

30 **B**

Revenue will be 1.50 million × 1.04 = USD 1.56 million this year i.e. GBP 0.945 million

(1.56/1.6500)

Assume cost of sales will stay constant (since sales volume stays constant) at GBP 0.67 million.

Then, gross profit margin will be [(0.945 − 0.67)/0.945] = 29.1%

31 **D**

Sustainability reporting (for example, looking at an organisation's economic, environmental and social impacts) is an important part of an integrated report. An integrated report would include details of sustainability, but also look at other issues as well (such as how the organisation creates value for their stakeholders)

32   A

It most regions there is no legal requirement to prepare an integrated report, it is voluntary. However, this may change in the future as <IR> becomes more popular and stakeholders demand more detailed information.

33   D

Whilst running a surplus will help to ensure the survival of Cleo, it may not be needed every year. If a charity always has a surplus then donors may feel that their money is not being used correctly.

All other actions meet one of the 3E's of improving value for money – Economy (bulk discount), Effectiveness (more accommodation) and Efficiency (property utilisation and occupation).

SYLLABUS SECTION B: SOURCES OF LONG-TERM FUNDS

34   B

Modigliani and Miller's 1963 gearing theory is the 'with tax' theory. It concludes that the cost of capital reduces as the gearing level increases.

35   C

The traditional view of gearing concludes that the cost of capital follows a U shaped curve, and therefore that there is an optimum gearing level at which the cost of capital is minimised and the value of the company is maximised.

36   A

Modigliani and Miller's formula is:

$$k_{adj} = k_{eu} \times [1 - (tL)]$$

where L is (D/(D+E)

Remember that (D+E) will change from \$1,770 million before the refinancing to \$1,710 million after the refinancing because of the tax shield on debt.

Explanation:
Because Vg = Vu +TD, the geared company's value is linked closely to the tax relief on debt interest.

We can calculate the new equity value as follows using Vg = Vu + TB

Currently: Vg = 1,770 (D+E) and D = 420.

Therefore Vg = Vu + TB is 1770 = Vu + (0.3 ×420)

Rearranging this gives a Vu of 1,644

After the change in gearing, Vu will still be 1,644 from above, but now D = 220.

Now Vg = Vu + TB is Vg = 1644 + (0.3 ×220).

Vg = 1,710 (made up of D = 220 and E = 1,490)

37 B

Modigliani and Miller's formula is:

$$k_{eg} = k_{eu} + [(k_{eu} - k_d) \times \left(V_D(1-t) \Big/ V_E \right)]$$

where k_d is the yield to the debt holders.

Therefore, the correct answer is the second one on the list.

38 C

Modigliani and Miller's formula is:

$$V_g = V_u + TD$$

Therefore, the value of the company if it funds the project using the bond is Vu (the value if the company continued to be all equity financed) plus 20% × $20 million (i.e. $4 million).

Vu can be found by discounting the earnings figure as a perpetuity.

So

$$V_u = \frac{30\,m}{0.15} = \$200\,m$$

Therefore, Vg = $200 million + $4 million = $204 million.

Finally, if the value of the company is $204 million, but this incorporates $20 million of debt, the equity value must be $184 million, the third answer on the list.

39 C

Interest is paid regardless of the performance of the company, providing a more predictable return for investors, lowering the risk of investment.

Tax deductibility is not relevant here, as M&M's 1958 model assumes no corporation tax.

40 C

Vg = Vu + TB

= $72m + ($36.2m × 0.33) = $83.946m

Less debt $36.2m = $47.746m

Divide by 10m shares = $4.77

(A) Forgot to divide by number of shares

(B) No tax effect

(D) Same as Co C

41 A

Keg = 17.5% + (17.5% − 7.5%) × [1(1 − 0.33)/2] = 20.85%

42 C

The return to shareholders becomes less variable when gearing is lower.

43   A

As gearing increases WACC first falls due to the lower cost of debt, but as k_e begins to increase rapidly, this dominates and WACC rises.

44   The answer is 8.8%

$K_{adj} = K_{eu} (1 - tL)$

$0.094 = K_{eu} (1 - 0.3 \times 0.2)$

$0.094 = K_{eu} \times 0.94$

$K_{eu} = 0.1$

$K_{adj} = 0.1 \times (1 - 0.3 \times 0.4)$

$WACC = 0.088 = 8.8\%$

45   D

$V_g = V_u + TB$

$V_g = 60 + 0.3 \times 20$

$V_g = 66$

$K_{adj} = K_{eu}(1 - tL)$

$K_{adj} = 0.15 (1 - 0.3 \times 20/66)$

$K_{adj} = 0.136 = 13.6\%$

46   The answer is 22.22%

$K_{eu} = 15\%$ (current WACC)

Required WACC = 14%

$K_{adj} = K_{eu} (1 - tL)$

$0.14 = 0.15 (1 - 0.3 \times L)$

$0.14 = 0.15 - 0.045L$

$0.045L = 0.01$

$L = 0.2222$

47   The answer is 6.4%

$K_{adj} = K_{eu} (1 - tL)$

$0.094 = K_{eu} (1 - 0.3 \times 0.2)$

$0.094 = 0.94 \times K_{eu}$

$K_{eu} = 0.1$

$K_{adj} = 0.1 \times (1 - 0.3 \times 0.4)$

$WACC = 0.088$

% change = (9.4 − 8.8)/9.4

48 The answer is **13.42%**

$K_{eg} = K_{eu} + (K_{eu} - K_d) \times D(1 - t)/E$

$0.14 = K_{eu} + (K_{eu} - 0.08) \times 8 \times 0.7/52$

$0.14 = K_{eu} + 0.1077(K_{eu} - 0.08)$

$0.14 = K_{eu} + 0.1077K_{eu} - 0.008616$

$0.1486 = 1.1077K_{eu}$

$0.1486/1.1077 = K_{eu} = 0.1342 = $ WACC

Note: WACC = K_{eu} for an ungeared company

49 The answer is **14.4%**

WACC = $k_{eu}(1 - tL)$

Where L = Debt/(Debt + Equity) = 1/5 = 0.2

So WACC = $0.15[1 - (0.2)(0.2)] = 0.144$ (14.4%)

50 The answer is **14.7%**

$k_{eg} = k_{eu} + (k_{eu} - K_d)(V_d/V_e)(1 - t)$

$0.14 = k_{eu} + (k_{eu} - 0.08)(0.4)(0.8)$

$0.14 = k_{eu} + (k_{eu} - 0.08)(0.32)$

$0.14 = k_{eu} + 0.32k_{eu} - 0.0256$

$1.32k_{eu} = 0.1656$

$k_{eu} = 0.12545$

Then, with new gearing level:

$k_{eg} = 0.12545 + (0.12545 - 0.08)(0.6)(0.8)$

$\quad = 0.14727$

Therefore: 14.7%

51   The answer is **$10.01**

			$m
$V_u = 10m \times 9.50$		=	95
			—
$V_g = V_u + TB$			
$V_g = 95 + 0.2(20)$		=	99
Less : Value of debt		=	(20)
			—
	V_e	=	79
			—

No. shares repurchased (20m/9.5)	=	2,105,263.16
No. shares remaining (10m – 20m/9.5)	=	7,894,736.84
Value per share (79m/7,894,736.84)	=	10.0067
	Therefore	**$10.01**

52   **C**

Bonds and shares are traded on both the Primary and Secondary markets.

53   The interest cover ratio must be higher than 3

The ratio of net debt to EBITDA must be lower than 3

An entity is perceived to be risky if its interest cover ratio is low and/or its net debt to EBITDA ratio is high.

54   **A**

The rest would increase gearing even further.

55   **A**

The correct answer is $15 million, being [$30 million – (10% × $50 million)] × 80%, minus the $5 million retained earnings limit. The post tax earnings will be [$30 million – (10% × $50 million)] × 80% = $20 million, so paying a dividend of $15 million would leave exactly $5 million as retained earnings (thus meeting the requirements of the covenant).

56   **B**

If leasing the relevant cash flows are the lease payments and the tax relief on these lease payments. As the lease payment is in advance, it will run from year 0 – 3 and the tax relief is one year in arrears, so will run from 2 – 5. The discount rate is 6%, being the post-tax cost of borrowing (8.57% × (1 – 0.30)).

Therefore, PV = [– $275,000 × (1 + 2.673)] + [$82,500 × (4.212 – 0.943)] = – $740,000

57   **C**

The asset costs $450,000. The total lease payments are $120,000 × 4 = $480,000, therefore interest charged is $30,000. Using the sum of the digits method, we have 4 × 5/2 = 10 (or for a 4 year period 4 + 3 + 2 + 1 = 10)

Year	Interest	Tax relief @30%
1	4/10 × 30,000 = 12,000	3,600
2	3/10 × 30,000 = 9,000	2,700
3	2/10 × 30,000 = 6,000	1,800
4	1/10 × 30,000 = 3,000	900

58   The answer is **$370,000**

Discount rate is post-tax cost of borrowing = 7.14% × (1 − 0.30) = 5%

Year	Cash flow	5% DR	PV
0	(500)	1	(500)
1 – 5	(500/5) × 30%	4.329	130
NPV			(370)

59   **C**

An investment bank would be able to organise all aspects of an IPO (including underwriting if necessary). A stockbroker would usually only deal with smaller issues and placings.

60   **D**

$$\frac{5 \times \$5 + 1 \times £3.50}{5 + 1} = \$4.75$$

61   **A**

A 1 for 3 rights issues will mean 5 million new shares will be issued. This will mean there will be 20 million shares in total after the rights issue.

If the TERP is $4.80, the total value of the company after the rights issue will be 20 million × $4.80 = $96 million

The value of the company cum-rights was 15 million × $5 = $75 million.

The value of finance raised must therefore be $96 million – $75 million = $21 million.

62   **C**

Answer (A) is a potential correct answer although it isn't necessary to offer a discount for this reason. Answer (D) would only be relevant if a rights issue was not successful and was followed by a new issue of shares.

If the market price of a share was to fall in the offer period, there is a risk that the rights issue will fail, as it would be cheaper to buy more shares in the market than it would to take up the offer under the rights issue. This is therefore the main reason why a discount would be offered.

63   D

If all the gain goes to existing shareholders, the market value of their shares will rise.

The new shares will have the same market value.

As there is no gain available for the new shareholders, they must have paid this (higher) market value for their shares.

64   The answer is **$1,500,000**

Current total MV (10m @$5)	50,000,000
Add: NPV	1,885,000
New funds raised	5,280,000
New total MV ($)	57,165,000
Existing number of shares	10,000,000
Add: New shares issued (5.28m/4.80)	1,100,000
New number of shares	11,100,000
MV per share	$5.15
Existing MV/cost	($5.00)
Gain per share	$0.15
Total gain	$1,500,000

65   The answer is **18.03%**

Current total MV	50,000,000
Add: NPV	2,440,000
New funds	5,280,000
New total MV	57,720,000
Existing number of shares	10,000,000
Add: New shares issued (5.28m/4.80)	1,100,000
New number of shares	11,100,000

	Shareholders		
	Existing	*New*	*Total*
MV per share	5.20	5.20	
Existing MV/cost	(5.00)	(4.80)	
Gain per share	0.20	0.40	
Total gain	2,000,000	440,000	2,440,000
Percentage	81.97%	18.03%	

66   The answer is **$2.60**

	$m
Current total MV (30m shares @ $2.50)	75
Add: Gain accruing to existing shareholders (=NPV)	3
New value of existing shares	78
=> Value per share (78m/30m)	**$2.60**

Since there is no gain available for the new investor, this must be the price he pays for his shares

67   The answer is **$0.39**

Current total MV	70,000,000
Add: NPV	1,151,000
New funds	2,835,000
New total MV	73,986,000
Existing number of shares	20,000,000
Add: New shares issued (2.835m/(3.50 × 0.9))	900,000
New number of shares	20,900,000
MV per share	3.54
Existing MV/cost	(3.15)
Gain per share	0.39

68   **C**

(A) is a result of assuming that a perfect capital market exists; it is not a conclusion

(B) is the Gordon growth model

(D) contradicts the dividend valuation model, which is not disputed by M&M

69   **A**

If a company announces that its long-term policy is to pay no dividends, the only investors in the shares should be investors seeking capital growth through reinvestment. Companies such as Microsoft have argued that shareholders needing cash can sell their shares in the market at any time, and so do not need dividends. The argument is also made that capital gains are not taxed until the shares are sold, which means that capital gains tax will be deferred, whereas tax on dividends would be an annual event. The tax treatment of capital gains is therefore favourable for investors seeking capital growth.

70   **A, B, E**

71   A, D

Debt may or may not be secured.

Interest returns are not guaranteed – for example if the company becomes bankrupt.

Transaction costs are assumed to be zero, a simplifying assumption of M&M's models.

72   A, D, E

Low returns on conserved cash will have a minimal impact on the share price.

There is no information given on other companies' performance.

The clientele (A) and signalling (E) effects both apply. Investors manufacturing dividends (D) will depress the share price.

73   Company X is planning on **decreasing** its dividend, but is concerned that the share price will fall.

This demonstrates the **signalling** effect.

74   A

The NPV of the project is equal to the increase in wealth of the shareholders (i.e. the increase in share price).

Therefore, an NPV of $6 million, split between 10 million shares means an increase of 6/10 = $0.60 per share.

75   A

Interest cover is (operating profit/interest payable)

= $305,000/[(10,000 × $100 × 4%) + ($500,000 × 2.5%)] = 5.8

76   B

Before the finance is raised:

Gearing = 100,000/(100,000 + (200,000 × $1.30)) = 27.8%

Interest cover = 25,000/(9% × 100,000) = 2.78

After the finance is raised:

Gearing = (100,000 + 40,000)/(100,000 + 40,000 + (200,000 × $1.25)) = 35.9%

Interest cover = 25,000/[(9% × 100,000) + (5% × 40,000)] = 2.27

77   B

The amount of cash required for the repurchase is 1 million shares at $0.40 each, so $0.40 million in total. Hence, cash will fall from $5 million to $4.6 million.

The new number of shares in issue will be (6 million – 1 million =) 5 million, so assuming that earnings stay constant, the EPS will be (total earnings/5 million).

Currently, earnings are $0.30 × 6 million = $1.80 million.

Therefore, EPS will be $1.80 million/5 million = $0.36 after the repurchase.

78   A, B

Debt

Interest = $60,000 and value of debt increases by $1m, so the ratios become:

Interest cover = (Earnings before interest and tax/Interest payable) = $1,600,000/$340,000 = 4.7 times

Earnings per share (EPS) = (Profit after tax/No. of shares) = $882,000/1,000,000 = $0.882

Note that profit after tax = (EBIT – Interest) × (1 – 0.30)

Gearing = (debt/equity) = $5m/$7m = 71.4%

Equity

250,000 extra shares and value of equity increases by $1m, so the ratios become:

Interest cover = (Earnings before interest and tax/Interest payable) = $1,600,000/$280,000 = 5.7 times

Earnings per share (EPS) = (Profit after tax/No. of shares) = $924,000/1,250,000 = $0.739

Gearing = (debt/equity) = $4m/$8m = 50.0%

79   C

Market value of debt is $50m × 0.99 = $49.5m

Current market value of equity is 40m × $3.14 = $125.6m, so after the share repurchase it will be $115.6m.

Therefore (D/(D+E)) = 49.5/(49.5 + 115.6) = 30.0%

80   C

Currently P/E is 8.55 and share price is $0.90.

Therefore, EPS = (0.90/8.55 =) $0.105

With 2 million shares in issue, this amounts to total earnings of approximately $210,000

After the issue, the project will add $50,000 earnings to this, so earnings will become $260,000.

Total shares will be 2 million existing shares + 1 million new ones (1 for 2 rights). Therefore 3 million in total.

Hence EPS will be 260,000/3 million = $0.087

81   C

Shareholder wealth is unaffected by a scrip dividend.

Consider a typical shareholder with 100 shares. Under the terms of the scrip dividend, this shareholder would receive an entitlement to one new share for every 10 held. That is, the right to acquire 10 new shares (where 10 = 100/10).

This may give the shareholder the illusion of increased 'value' as he now holds 110 shares. However, the company itself has not changed in value and so the total value that those shares represent is unchanged.

Therefore, the value of each share after the scrip issue will be ($1.65 × 100)/110 = $1.50

82   B

Debt will rise to $6.2m + $3m = $9.2m.

Equity will rise (because of the extra value generated by the takeover) to

$4m + $6.1m + $0.6m = $10.7m

Therefore, [D/(D+E)] = 9.2/(9.2 + 10.7) = 46.2%

83   A

Interest cover = 8.3m/(1m + (8% × 8m)) = 5.06 times

Capital gearing ratio

Debt = 10m + 8m + 5m = $23m

Equity = 20m + 4m + 5m + 6m = $35m

D/(D+E) = 23m/(23m + 35m) × 100 = 39.7%

SYLLABUS SECTION C: FINANCIAL RISKS

84   C

A currency appreciates when it rises in value relative to another foreign currency. Likewise, a currency depreciates when it falls in value relative to another foreign currency. An appreciation in value of a currency makes that country's goods more expensive to residents of other countries. The depreciation of the value of a currency makes a country's goods more attractive to foreign buyers.

85   A, B, D, E

The only factor given that does not directly affect the demand for or supply of a currency is developments in IT.

86   A

Translation risk relates to the movement in value of assets and liabilities when preparing accounts.

87   C

The Canadian supplier is unaffected as it invoices in its local currency, the Canadian dollar. It will receive the same number of Canadian dollars regardless of any movements of the CAD against the GBP. Eady Co will have to pay more GBP to purchase the CAD payable, so will suffer a loss on the weakening of the GBP.

88   C

Political risk is the possibility of an unexpected politically motivated event in a country affecting the outcome of an investment. Political risk analysis will consider the differences between the home and target country, e.g. the stability of government, corruption by officials, different religious beliefs or ethnic tensions.

89   D

Interest rate risk is the probability of an increase in interest rates causing a bond's price to decrease.

90   D

Interest is tax deductible; therefore, the firm's cost of debt would be the percentage cost of the bonds less the tax effect.

91   A, B, D, E

A – Assets in the foreign currency can be offset against the liabilities in the same currency

B – Interest costs will be payable in the foreign currency and can be paid from the income in the same currency – i.e. this allows for netting to occur. Netting is a form of internal hedging mitigating transaction risk.

C – False – Simply having a foreign loan does not reduce the downside risk of interest rates increasing.

D – The stability and state of the local banking system may limit local financing.

E – Raising finance locally may also help to maintain the interest of the local government in the success of the business, and there is less risk that the assets will be confiscated.

92   A

The H\$ is the base currency and the EUR is the variable, so the forward rate is

$6.250 \times (1.02/1.06) = 6.014$

93   C

The GBP is the base currency and the EUR is the variable, so the forward rate is

$1.2400 \times (1.0075/1.005) = 1.2431$

94   B

$1.2075 \times (1.02)^2 = 1.2563$

95   D

The W\$ is the base currency and the EUR is the variable, so the future expected rate is

$1.9900 \times (1.01/1.08) = 1.8610$

Therefore, the value of the transaction is EUR 100,000/1.8610 = W\$ 53,735

96   C

The C\$ is the base currency and the USD is the variable, so the future expected rate is

$1.1144 \times (1.015/1.025) = 1.1035$ (need to pro rate interest rates by 6/12th as need the 6 month rate, so 3% × 6/12 = 1.5% and 5% × 6/12 = 2.5%)

97   D

Inflation rates are not relevant to Interest Rate Parity theory (they are relevant to Purchasing Power Parity Theory).

98   7.0%

If the International Fisher effect is true, then the real rate of return in each country should be the same and hence the differences in interest rates can be explained purely due to the differences in inflation.

In Country A the real rate is given by

$1 + r = (1 + m)/(1 = i) = 1.113/1.05 = 1.06$, so r = 6%

Rearranging this equation for Country B,

$1+i = (1 + m)/(1 + r) = 1.1342/1.06 = 1.07$, so i = 7%

99 $707 MILLION

The Z value for a one-tail 95% confidence level is 1.645 (from the Normal Distribution tables).

VaR = standard deviation × Z value, so the

VaR = USD 430 million × 1.645 = 707.35 which rounds to 707.

100   1-DAY VAR = GBP 115,000

USD 10,000,000/1.2785 = GBP 7,821,666

Std Dev = 7,821,666 × 0.75% = GBP 58,662.50

Z score for 97.5% = 1.96 (from tables)

VAR = GBP 58,662.50 × 1.96 = GBP 114,978.5

5-DAY VAR = GBP 257,140

5 day VaR = 1 day VaR × $\sqrt{5}$ = GBP 115,000 × 2.236 = GBP 257,140

101   C

Leading with the payment eliminates the foreign currency exposure by removing the liability. Borrowing short-term in Euros to meet the payment obligation in three months' time matches assets and liabilities and provides cover against the exposure. A forward exchange contract is a popular method of hedging against exposure.

102

Internal	External
Leading and lagging	Forward contracts
Matching and netting	Futures
Countertrade	Options

103

Method	Example
Matching	Financing a foreign investment with a foreign currency loan
Netting	Using a foreign currency receipt to offset a foreign currency payment
Pooling	Transferring all bank account balances in one currency into a single account
Countertrade	Exchanging goods or services of similar value

104 A

(1) The company can buy GBP 500,000 for USD 950,000 compared to USD 975,000 on the spot market.

(2) The company can sell the GBP 400,000 for SGD 1,160,000 compared to SGD 1,180,000 on the spot market.

The call option should be exercised but the put option should not be exercised.

105 A

First calculate the number of contracts using the STRIKE price so

USD 5m/1.6 = GBP 3,125,000 then at a contract size of GBP 25,000.

SGB will take an option on GBP 3,125,000/25000 = 125 contracts.

The premium is USD 1,000 per contract so USD 125,000 as a premium must be paid to the exchange when the contract is taken out so this transaction will be done at the current spot of 1.5500.

125,000/1.5500 = GBP 80,645.

106 32,531

X will be looking to buy USD so the starting point is the spot rate of 1.5400.

You need to subtract a premium so the forward rate = 1.5400 − 0.0030 = 1.5370.

GBP cost = 50,000/1.5370 = 32,531.

107 849,000

The hedge requires X to borrow in GBP, translate to EUR and deposit EUR. The deposit (plus interest) can then be used to pay the supplier.

A payment of EUR 1 million in 6 months will require a EUR deposit (earning 1% interest over six months) now of 1,000,000/1.01 = EUR 990,099.

Using a spot rate of 1.1950 this requires X to borrow 990,099/1.1950 = GBP 828,535. This is borrowed at an interest rate of 2.5% for six months.

Repayment of the loan will cost X 828,535 × 1.025 = GBP 849,248 (so 849,000 to the nearest GBP 1,000).

108 USD 41,835,000

DWTV will need to BUY GBP to pay the UK supplier and will want to pay the lowest price per GBP i.e. 1.6700. So exercise the option.

Note: At 1.6700, GBP 25m would cost USD 41,750,000 whereas at 1.6850 it would cost USD 42,125,000.

However DWTV will also have paid the premium of USD 85,000, taking the total cost to 41,750,000 + 85,000 = 41,835,000.

109 D

As SOMH is due to receive EUR, it will be selling & the bank buying, therefore the higher rate is used: 1.7027

There is a discount of 2.5 cents (0.0250 EUR), which will be added to the spot rate as EUR will be less valuable in the future.

1.7027 + 0.0250 = 1.7277

700,000/1.7277 = 405,162.93

110 GBP 798,044

If APS exercises the option it will receive EUR 1,200,000/1.4405 = GBP 833,044.08

If APS sells the EUR on the spot market, they will receive EUR 1,200,000/1.4640 = 819,672.13

The option is therefore 'in the money' and so APS will exercise the option.

The premium was GBP 35,000, so the net receipt (to the nearest GBP) is:

833,044 – 35,000 = GBP 798,044

111 D

We need the contract size and the transaction in GBP, use the strike price

USD 4,000,000/1.4500 = GBP 2,758,621 (if you chose C you used the spot rate)

Now we work out the number of contracts:

2,758,621/25,000 = 110.34484

So that's 111 contracts (if you chose B you rounded down)

At USD 2,500 per contract this would cost USD 277,500, but we need the cost in GBP (if you chose A you stopped too early)

USD 277,500/1.2750 = **GBP 217,647**

We use the spot as the transaction is taking place today.

112

Instrument	Description
A Forward Rate Agreement (FRA)	An over the counter instrument, with a fixed rate
B Interest Rate Guarantee (IRG)	An over the counter instrument, hedging only downside risk
C Future	A traded instrument, with a fixed rate
D Option	A traded instrument, hedging only downside risk

113 6.20%

The reference rate of 6.00% is higher than the FRA rate of 5.70% (banks sell high, remember) so the FRA will be settled by a payment to X of 0.30%.

The actual rate paid on the loan is 6.50% (base plus 0.50%), and deducting the FRA receipt of 0.30% gives an effective rate of 6.20%.

114 A

An interest-rate cap will pay its owner the maximum of zero or the market rate minus the cap rate, times the notional principal. An interest rate cap is a bundle of interest rate calls with successive expiry dates, whereas an interest rate floor is a bundle of interest rate puts.

115 C

Investors 'close out' their positions and therefore either win or lose cash.

116 B

OTC derivative contracts (securities) are customized and have poor liquidity.

The contract is with a specific counterparty and there is default risk since there is no clearing house to guarantee performance.

117 A

The existence of derivatives markets does not affect the level of interest rates. The other statements are true.

118 C, E, F

Options do not provide complete certainty as to the amount paid or received as they may or may not be exercised but they do ensure that the cash flows associated with financing the transaction are known in advance as the premium has to be paid up front regardless of what happens. This is in contrast with futures where there is some variation in cash flows associated with the transaction as variation margin may have to be paid. They are far from being simple, cheap or easy to understand but they are very useful for hedging uncertain transactions as they are a right and not an obligation to do something. In other words they need not be exercised.

119 B

As the loan starts in 6 months, they will use the 6 v 15 option at 3.45 – 3.7.

As they are taking out a loan the bank will be charging them the higher rate, 3.7%.

As it's L IBOR+ 0.55 and the FRA is at 3.7%, the company will pay 3.7 + 0.55 = 4.25%.

120 D

There is a bigger difference in the variable rates so to take advantage of this, B will borrow variable and A then has to borrow at a fixed rate. Use L% to get B on fixed and A on variable. Then 3.5% is the balancing figure to split the saving on an equal basis.

It would work out like:

	Co A	Co B
Paid to bank	(7%)	(L+2%)
A pays B	(L)	L
B pays A	3.5%	(3.5%)
Net effect	(L+3.5%)	(5.5%)

121 A, B, D

Interest rate swaps can be used to protect the fair value of fixed rate debt instruments, not floating rate debt instruments.

122 C

DD Co pays LIBOR + 1.5% at the moment and the bank has offered a swap at the rate of 5% for LIBOR (i.e. DD Co will pay 5% to the bank in exchange for LIBOR).

Hence the net rate is (LIBOR + 1.5%) + 5% – LIBOR = 6.5%

23 A, B, E, F

A   Selling FRAs protects Tither from interest rate falls by fixing the rate they will receive.

B   Tither matches its assets and liabilities to have a common interest rate (i.e. loan and investment both have floating rates).

C   Options to sell STIRs will protect against interest rate rises but allow Tither to benefit from any falls, so would be appropriate for a loan.

D   Buying an interest rate cap will protect against interest rate rises, as Tither are depositing they would want interest rates to rise, so this is inappropriate.

E   Buying bond futures is appropriate as Tither is looking to deposit funds.

F   Tither will try to maintain a certain balance between its fixed rate and floating rate borrowing. The portfolio of fixed and floating rate debts thus provide a natural hedge against changes in interest rates. There will be less exposure to the adverse effects of each but there will also be less exposure to any favourable movements in the interest rate.

124 A

The hedge requires H to borrow in GBP today, translate to USD and deposit USD. The deposit (plus interest) can then be used to pay the supplier the USD 2.5m owed.

A payment of USD 2.5m in 9 months will require a USD deposit (earning 2.6%pa × 9/12 = 1.95% interest over nine months) now of 2.5m/1.0195 = USD 2,452,182. Remember to add 1.95%, we multiply by 1.0195, so to work backwards we must divide by 1.0195.

Using a spot rate of 1.2260 (need to BUY USD to place them on deposit) this requires H to borrow 2,452,182/1.2260 = GBP 2,000,148. This is borrowed at an interest rate of 4%pa × 9/12 = 3% for nine months.

Repayment of the loan will cost H GBP 2,000,148 × 1.03 = GBP 2,060,152 (so **GBP 2,060,000** to the nearest GBP 1,000).

125 B

The hedge requires J to borrow in CAD today, translate to GBP and deposit GBP. The CAD 1.7m received from the Canadian customer will then be used to pay off the Canadian loan in full (loan plus 4 months' interest).

The receipt of CAD 1.7m in 4 months will pay off a loan today (costing 3.3%pa × 4/12 = 1.1% interest over four months) of CAD 1.7m/1.011 = CAD 1,681,503. Remember to add 1.1%, we multiply by 1.011, so to work backwards we must divide by 1.011.

Using a spot rate of 1.7580 (need to SELL CAD received from the Canadian loan) this gives J 1,681,503/1.7580 = GBP 956,486. This is deposited in the UK at an interest rate of 2.1%pa × 4/12 = 0.7% for four months.

In four months' time the deposit will mature and H will receive GBP 956,486 × 1.007 = GBP 963,181 (so **GBP 963,000** to the nearest GBP 1,000).

126 C

The hedge requires Q to borrow in GBP today, translate to EUR and deposit EUR. The GBP 1.2m received from the UK customer will then be used to pay off the GBP loan in full (loan plus 6 months' interest).

The receipt of GBP 1.2m in 6 months will pay off a loan today (costing 4.0%pa × 6/12 = 2% interest over six months) of GBP 1.2m/1.02 = GBP 1,176,471. Remember to add 2%, we multiply by 1.02, so to work backwards we must divide by 1.02.

Using a spot rate of 1.1000 (need to BUY EUR using the GBP from the UK loan) this gives Q GBP 1,176,471 × 1.1000 = EUR 1,294,118. This is deposited in France at an interest rate of 2.4%pa × 6/12 = 1.2% for four months.

In six months' time the deposit will mature and Q will receive EUR 1,294,118 × 1.012 = EUR 1,309,647 (so **EUR 1,310,000** to the nearest GBP 1,000).

127 B, D, H

A deposit will require the company to BUY the futures now (remember: Deposit = Buy, Loan = Sell). The loan will start at the end of May. As we don't have May futures, we need to choose futures with an expiry date AFTER this – so June futures.

The number of contracts = (Amount/contract size) × (length of deposit / length of contracts)

The number of contracts = ($3.5m/$500k) × (5 months / 3 months) = 11.7 = 12 contracts (just round to the nearest number)

So the company will need to **BUY 12 June futures.**

128 A

- Buy or sell futures? Sell, since we are borrowing

- Number of contracts = (Amount/contract size) × (length of deposit / length of contracts) = ($3,300,000/£500,000) × 6 months/3 months = 13.2 = 13 contracts

- Which expiry date? September contracts – closely matches the transaction date of 20th September.

Contact the exchange: We need to sell 13 September contracts at a price of 93.55 (remember this corresponds to an interest rate of 100 – 93.55 = 6.45%

Two months later:

Transaction: Interest will be $3.3m × 6/12 × 8% = $132,000

Futures market:

- Gain per contract = SELL at 93.55, now close out so BUY at 92.13 = (93.55 – 92.13) = 1.42%

- Total gain is 1.42% × 13 contracts × ($500,000 × 3/12) = $23,075

Hence, net cost = $132,000 – $23,075 = **$108,925**

(i.e. a net interest rate of 6.6% – this was not a perfect hedge due to rounding the number of contracts and a small amount of basis risk).

129 A

D will need to sell the USD it receives so the relevant spot rate is 1.4820 (remember – buy at lower rate and sell at the higher rate). The forward is at a DISCOUNT, so we must ADD this to the spot rate (remember – add a discount and subtract a premium). Therefore the relevant forward rate will be 1.4820 + 0.026 (2.6 cents) = 1.5080.

So the final receipt will be USD 450,000 / 1.5080 = **GBP 298,408**

130 D

E will need to buy the EUR it needs to pay the supplier so the relevant spot rate is 1.0986 (remember – buy at lower rate and sell at the higher rate). The forward is at a PREMIUM, so we must SUBTRACT this from the spot rate (remember – add a discount and subtract a premium). Therefore the relevant forward rate will be 1.0986 – 0.015 (1.5 cents) = 1.0836.

So the final receipt will be EUR 285,000 / 1.0836 = **GBP 263,012**

131 B, D, F

The UK company will need to sell USD and buy GBP when it receives the USD 2.85m to convert it into GBP (their home currency). Since the futures contracts are in GBP (the size is GBP 62,500), and the company wants to buy GBP, they should BUY futures contracts to set it up.

The money is due to be received in August so September futures should be used (go later than the transaction date).

The number of contracts = (Amount/contract size). However the amount is in USD and the contract size is in GBP, therefore the amount (or the contract size – it doesn't matter which) needs to be converted at the current relevant futures price – 1.5200

The number of contracts = (USD 2.85m/1.5200) / GBP 62,500 = 30 contracts

So the company will need to **BUY 30 September** futures.

132 D

The UK company will need to buy EUR and sell GBP to pay the Spanish supplier the EUR 1m due. Since the futures contracts are in GBP (the size is GBP 62,500), and the company wants to sell GBP, they should SELL futures contracts to set it up.

The money is due to be received in June so June futures should be used.

The number of contracts = (Amount/contract size). However the amount is in EUR and the contract size is in GBP, therefore the amount (or the contract size – it doesn't matter which) needs to be converted at the current relevant (June) futures price – 1.1800

The number of contracts = (EUR 1m/1.1800) / GBP 62,500 = 13.6 contracts = 14 contracts

So the company will need to sell 14 June futures.

When the company closes out the contracts on the 22nd June there will be a **LOSS** of 0.0065 (Sell at 1.1800, Buy at the current futures price of 1.1865) per contract.

This gives a total loss of 0.0065 × 14 contracts × 62,500 (contract size) = EUR 5,688.

This loss then needs converting into GBP at the spot rate on 22nd June: 5,688 / 1.1785 = **GBP 4,826**

133 B

On 1st October:

T will need to buy USD and sell EUR to pay the US supplier the USD 5m due. Since the futures contracts are in EUR (the size is EUR 62,500), and the company wants to sell EUR, they should SELL futures contracts to set it up.

The money is due to be received in December so December futures should be used.

The number of contracts = (Amount/contract size). However the amount is in USD and the contract size is in EUR, therefore the amount (or the contract size – it doesn't matter which) needs to be converted at the current (1st October) futures price – 1.1530

The number of contracts = (USD 5m/1.1530) / EUR 250,000 = 17.3 contracts = 17 contracts

So the company will need to sell 17 December futures.

On 17th December:

T will need to go and buy the USD 5m at the new spot rate, costing: USD 5m / 1.1260 = EUR 4,440,497.

When the company closes out the contracts on the 17th December there will be a GAIN of 0.0190 (Sell at 1.1530, Buy at the 17th December futures price of 1.1340) per contract.

This gives a total gain of 0.0190 × 17 contracts × 250,000 (contract size) = USD 80,750.

This loss then needs converting into EUR at the spot rate on 17th December: 80,750 / 1.1260 = EUR 71,714

Net cost = 4,440,497 less gain of 71,714 = **EUR 4,368,783**

Note: This question is longer and more complicated than those likely to be seen in the exam, however any part of this question could be tested.

134 A

JPY 227m/107.8 = USD 2,105,751

Std Dev = 2,105,751 × 0.62% = USD 13,056

Z score for 96% = 1.75 (from the tables. This is technically for 95.99% but close enough)

1 day VAR = USD 13,056 × 1.75 = USD 22,848

7 day VaR = 1 day VaR × $\sqrt{7}$ = USD 22,848 × 2.6458 = **USD 60,450** = USD 60,000 to nearest thousand

135 C

Changes to exchange rates between the date of the transaction (sale/purchase) and the date of payment is transaction risk. Here M is concerned the Australian dollar will depreciate, reducing the value of the receipt in the home currency.

SYLLABUS SECTION D: BUSINESS VALUATION

136 A, D, E

The other points are reasons for a sell-off.

137 C

Asset stripping occurs when it is thought that the company is incorrectly valued and that the value of the assets is actually greater than the market capitalisation, and that the company could be purchased, broken up and the assets sold off for a profit.

138 A, B, D

After the management buyout, there are likely to be fewer economies of scale (C) as Spring Co is no longer part of a larger entity.

Although Spring Co no longer has to pay dividends to Season Co (E), it will now have to satisfy the bank and the venture capitalist, so there may be little difference in the overall amounts paid out.

139 D

The rate of return on equity is greater than that on debt, so venture capitalists like to provide finance in the form of equity. However, too much equity (more than the managers themselves have put in) would mean that the venture capitalists would control the business – a situation that would be unacceptable to the managers. Therefore, venture capitalists generally provide some equity finance to take a significant minority stake (e.g. 40% – 49%) and then provide the rest of the required funds in the form of debt finance.

140 B

The larger company uses its increased size and bargaining power to access cheaper debt finance.

141 A

Both companies operate in the same industry, even though they are in different countries. They are competitors and this is a horizontal acquisition.

142 B

143 C

Herra is purchasing a company that retails products that it manufactures. This is Vertical Integration.

144 C

The regulator is there to ensure that any proposed take-over is not anti-competitive and does not cause damage to the stakeholders.

145 D

The others are all post-bid defences.

146 B, D

A spin-off does not generate any cash (A), or involve paying cash back to shareholders (C). A MBO, not a spin-off, involves managers taking control (E).

147 C, D, E

(A) and (B) are post-bid defences.

148 B

Bootstrapping is a financial synergy.

149 B

150 C

Buying a controlling interest in a company, often from shareholders with little inclination to sell, requires a premium to be paid on acquisition (B and D). If there are likely to be synergies a premium can be paid without putting the wealth of the acquiring company's shareholders at risk.

151 B, C, D

(A) is false because this is horizontal, not vertical integration.

(E) is not a good reason for acquisition. Shareholders can diversify their own portfolios far more efficiently than companies can.

152 A

In a strongly efficient market, the prices would have moved BEFORE the information was made public. The markets here seem to be semi-strongly efficient.

153 A

Competition authorities can block a takeover (B) or allow it to proceed (C). Sometimes conditions are imposed on the takeover, but these would apply to the public interest (D) rather than the value of the bid (A) which is perceived as being purely a matter for the two companies' shareholders.

154 D

The cost of capital is irrelevant when considering the likely profitability of a company.

155 B

The regulators will be interested in matters relating to the public interest and competition. They will have no interest in commercial factors, or what the directors of TT think of the takeover.

156 B

The DVM formula gives $0.60 \times 1.10/(0.13 - 0.10) = \$22.00$

But the quoted share price for a share that is just about to pay a dividend will be cum – dividend, i.e. $\$22.00 + \$0.60 = \$22.60$

157 C

Equity value = P/E ratio × Post-tax profit = $8 \times [3.5m - (2m \times 10\%)](1 - 0.25) = \$19.8$ million

158 B

Expected value of FFF and GGG combined is:

9.5 × (5m + 3m + 0.5m) = $80.75 million

GGG's current value is

10 × 5m = $50 million.

Therefore the value of FFF to GGG is the difference between these two figures, i.e. $30.75 million.

159 B

The definition of free cash flow to equity is 'Cash flow from operations after deducting interest, tax, preference dividends and ongoing capital expenditure, but excluding capital expenditure associated with strategic acquisitions and/or disposals and ordinary share dividends.'

	$000
Operating profit	879
Interest	(210)
Taxable profit	669
Tax at 22%	(147)
Profit after tax	522
Add: Depreciation	167
Investment in NCA	(378)
Investment in WC	(143)
FREE CASH FLOW TO EQUITY	168

160 D

One way of valuing the equity of a firm is to forecast the free cash flows to equity and then discount at the cost of equity.

The definition of free cash flow to equity is 'Cash flow from operations after deducting interest, tax, preference dividends and ongoing capital expenditure, but excluding capital expenditure associated with strategic acquisitions and/or disposals and ordinary share dividends.'

Thus (A) is not correct as dividends should not be deducted and (C) is not correct as taxation should be deducted.

An alternative way of valuing the equity is to value the whole entity (debt + equity) and then subtract the market value of debt to be left with the market value of equity. With this method we would discount post-tax cash flows BEFORE financing charges (i.e. free cash flows to all investors) using the WACC to get the value of the entity. Then we would deduct the MV of the debt to get the MV of the equity.

(B) is nearly correct then, but it should be free cash flows to all investors being discounted not free cash flows to equity.

161 B

Forecast post-tax cash flows before financing charges should be discounted at WACC to give the value of the entity, and then the value of debt should be deducted to give the value of equity.

	T1	T2	T3	T4
$m	283	291	298	305
12%	0.893	0.797	0.712	0.636
PV	253	232	212	194

Value of the perpetuity from T5 to perpetuity is:

$[(305 \times 1.03)/(0.12 - 0.03)] \times 0.636 = 2,220$

Value of the entity = $3,111m (The sum of the PVs)

And therefore the value of the equity (70%) is $2,178m

162 A

$23.12m(1.05)/(0.12 - 0.05) = $346.80m

163 C

$1.5m(1.04)/(0.14 - 0.04) = $15.6 million. There are 1 million shares, so $15.60 per share.

164 C

A high P/E ratio often indicates that a high rate of growth of earnings is expected from a company.

165 C

P/E ratio = Share price/Earnings per share

Earnings per share is calculated as profit after tax after the deduction of preference share dividends = $17,000 – $2,000 = $15,000/70,000 = 21.4c per share.

= 204/21.4

= 9.5

166 B

Answer (A) is possible but only for companies with a temporary dip in profits. Answer (C) is also possible but the EMH implies that all shares are correctly priced and so a share cannot be 'overpriced'.

167 D

The dividend yield is 2% and the dividend cover is 4.

Dividend yield = Dividend/Share price

Dividend cover = Earnings/Dividends

Therefore earnings as a percentage of share price = dividend yield × dividend cover

Therefore earnings are (2% × 4) = 8% of the price.

The price must be 100/8 × 20 cents = 250 cents

168 B

The dividend per share is 2c

As the dividend cover is 4, the earnings per share are 8c

The price per share is thus 10 × 8c = 80c

There are $2 million of 25c shares = 8 million shares so the market value is 8 million × 80c = $6.4 million

169 C

$500,000/$0.25 × $2.30 = $4,600,000

170 D

As the company intends to list on the market, the shareholders are entitled to receive future dividends and hence the dividend valuation model is the correct method to use in this case.

171 The answer is **$0.102m**

((4.10 + 1.30) × 42%) + 0.32 + (0.45 × 72%) less (0.66 + 2.15) = $0.102m

172 The answer is

EPS	$3.71
Value per share using dividend valuation model	$36.23
Value per share using the P/E model	$42.67

Workings:

EPS = $11.12m/3m = $3.71

Dividend Valuation Model:

$g = rb$

$r = k_e = 11\%$ or 0.11

$b = (11.12 - 3.34)/11.12 = 0.70$

$g = 0.11 × 0.70 = 0.077$

Dividend per share = $3.34m/3m = $1.11

$P_o = \$1.11(1.077) /(0.11 - 0.077) = \$36.23$

P/E Valuation

P/E ratio of Zudun Co is $598m/$52m = 11.5

$P_o = \$3.71 × 11.5 = \$42.67$

173 B

Total value is $259,000 × 14 = $3,626,000

Value per share is $3,626,000/1m = $3.63

174 C

Dividend cover = earnings/dividends

So Earnings = dividends × dividend cover

Abbott Co earnings = $2m × 5 = $10m

Total value = 10 × $10m = $100m

175 A

The sale of land cannot happen again and the profit after tax used in the valuation must be sustainable for the future. Therefore we need to first remove the land profit from the profit after tax.

Sustainable profit after tax = 1.5 − 0.325 = $1.175 million

Total value of equity = 8 × $1.175 million = $9.4 million

176 B

The total value is $800,000 × 10 = $8 million, but this needs to be reduced for non-marketability as an unlisted company is not worth as much as a listed company.

In this case we need to reduce by 25%

Value of Veena Co = $8 million × 75% = $6 million

177 B

The current profit after tax needs to be adjusted for the directors' salaries to give a sustainable earnings figure for the valuation.

The after tax cost of the salaries is $40,000 × (1 − 0.30) = $28,000

So the adjusted earnings is $500,000 − $28,000 = $472,000

Total value is $472,000 × 5 = $2,360,000

178 C

Strong form market efficiency assumes that all information, both public and private, is reflected in a company's share price.

As the expansion strategy had been planned internally for a period of months, this private information would be included in the share price.

179 C

The preferred approach is a good spread of shares, as this minimises the risk in the portfolio and should ensure that Miss Coates does achieve something approaching the average return for the market.

180 B

181 The answer is

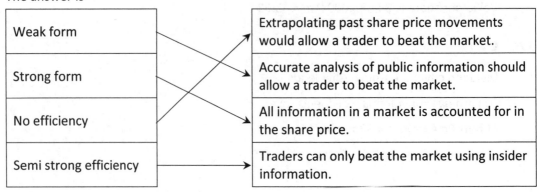

182 D

1   The expected NPV of a project has nothing to do with the efficiency of the market. Even though, with strong-form efficiency, a project's positive NPV is incorporated within the share price as soon as the project is devised and accepted, this does not deny the fact that the project has a positive NPV. Hence the existence of projects with a positive expected NPV neither supports nor contradicts the idea that the market is strong-form efficient. Therefore, false.

2   Strong-form efficiency states that the share price already includes all relevant information when a dividend is declared and the dividend adds no information. Therefore, false.

183 A

Current pre-tax profit generated from the intangibles is 453 – (1268 × 15%) = 262.8 ($000)

Assuming this value is a pre-tax cash flow occurring from T1 until perpetuity and discounted at the company WACC is (262.8(1 – 0.30))/0.11 = $1.672m

184 A

First of all we need to find a suitable ungeared beta

De-gear

$\beta_u = \beta_g \times E/(E + D(1 - t))$

$\beta_u = 1.8 \times 50/(50 + 50(1 - 0.30))$

$\beta_u = 1.06$

Then use this to find an appropriate β_g

$\beta_u = \beta_g \times E/(E + D(1 - t))$

$1.06 = \beta_g \times 60/(60 + 40(1 - 0.30))$

$1.06 = \beta_g \times 0.682$

$B_g = 1.06/0.682 = 1.55$

Use CAPM

$K_{eg} = R_f + \beta(R_m - Rf)$

$K_{eg} = 0.05 + 1.55 (0.08 - 0.05) = 9.65\%$

185 B

$(0.333)(0.06) + (0.333)(0.10) + 0.333(.05) = 0.07$

186 A

De-gear

$\beta_u = \beta_g \times E/(E + D(1 - t))$

$\beta_u = 0.9 \times 2/(2 + 0.7)$

$\beta_u = 0.6667$

Use CAPM

$K_{eu} = R_f + \beta_u (R_m - R_f)$

$K_{eu} = 2 + 0.6667 \times (8 - 2)$

$K_{eu} = 6.00\%$

187 D

Re-gear

$\beta_u = \beta_g \times E/(E + D(1 - t))$

$0.9 = \beta_g \times 2/(2.7)$

$B_g = 1.215$

Use CAPM

$K_{eg} = R_f + \beta(R_m - R_f)$

$K_{eg} = 2 + 1.215 \times 8$

$K_{eg} = 11.72\%$

188 B

Use CAPM

$K_{eg} = R_f + \beta(R_m - R_f)$

$K_{eg} = 2\% + 0.9 \times 8\%$

$K_{eg} = 9.20\%$

189 C

Re-gear

$\beta_u = \beta_g \times E/(E + D(1 - t))$

$0.9 = \beta_g \times 2/(2.7)$

$B_g = 1.215$

Use CAPM

$K_{eg} = R_f + \beta(R_m - R_f)$

$K_{eg} = 2 + 1.215 \times (8 - 2)$

$K_{eg} = 9.29\%$

190 A

Use CAPM

$K_{eg} = R_f + \beta(R_m - R_f)$

$K_{eg} = 2\% + 0.9 \times (8\% - 2\%)$

$K_{eg} = 7.40\%$

191 C

$$\beta_g = \beta_u + \left[(\beta_u - \beta_d) \left(\frac{Ve\,(1-t)}{Vd} \right) \right]$$

where Ve and Vd are the equity and debt values for our company (SIX Co in this case), and βu is the ungeared equity beta of APPLE Co, calculated as:

$$\beta_u = \left[1.45 \times \frac{70}{70 + 30\,(1-0.25)} \right] + \left[0.10 \times \frac{30\,(1-0.25)}{70 + 30\,(1-0.25)} \right] = 1.12$$

The correct answer is the third on the list.

192 B

If all the companies are facing the same business risk then their asset betas will be the same. The only difference for the equity beta will be the level of financial risk that they cause their shareholders. The gearing of Tarte Co is higher than company B's, but lower than company A's and so Tarte Co's equity beta will be between the two.

193 A

First of all we need to find a suitable ungeared beta

De-gear

$\beta_u = \beta_g \times E/(E + D(1 - t))$

$\beta_u = 1.2 \times 70/(70 + 30(1 - 0.30)$

$\beta_u = 0.92$

Then use this to find an appropriate βg

$\beta_u = \beta_g \times E/(E + D(1 - t))$

$0.92 = \beta_g \times 85/(85 + 15(1 - 0.30))$

$0.92 = \beta_g \times 0.890$

$B_g = 0.92/0.890 = 1.034$

Use CAPM

$K_{eg} = R_f + \beta(R_m - R_f)$

$K_{eg} = 0.04 + 1.034(0.10 - 0.04) = 10.2\%$

Therefore WACC = $(10.2\% \times 85/100) + (4\% \times (1 - 0.30) \times 15/100) = 9.1\%$

194 B

First of all we need to de-gear the current equity beta

De-gear

$\beta_u = \beta_g \times E/(E + D(1 - t))$

$\beta_u = 1.4 \times 70/(70 + 30(1 - 0.3))$

$\beta_u = 1.08$

This will then be used in the cost of equity

$K_{eu} = R_f + \beta_u(R_m - R_f)$

$K_{eu} = 0.05 + 1.08 \times 0.07$

$K_{eu} = 12.6\%$

195 C

First of all we need to find a suitable ungeared beta

De-gear

$\beta_u = \beta_g \times E/(E + D(1 - t))$

$\beta_u = 1.6 \times 80/(80 + 20(1 - 0.3))$

$\beta_u = 1.36$

Then use this to find an appropriate βg

$\beta_u = \beta_g \times E/(E + D(1 - t))$

$1.36 = \beta_g \times 70/(70 + 30(1 - 0.30))$

$1.36 = \beta_g \times 0.769$

$B_g = 1.36/0.769 = 1.77$

Use CAPM

$K_{eg} = R_f + \beta(R_m - Rf)$

$K_{eg} = 0.04 + 1.77(0.08 - 0.04) = 11.1\%$

196 A

The VC is making a $15 million equity investment. To generate a return of 20% a year on a compound basis this investment will need to grow to $25.92 million (= $15 million × $(1.20)^3$) at the end of 3 years.

The VC investment represents 37.5% (= 15/(15 + 25) × 100%) of the equity, therefore the total equity value will need to be $69.12 million (= $25.92 million/0.375).

197 C, D, E

198 B

A cash offer funded by debt would increase A's gearing (C) and would prevent the B shareholders from participating in the future growth of the company (D).

Since no A shares are being issued, the control of A's shareholders would stay the same (A).

199 D

Value of merged company ($ million) = 30 + 10 + 6 + 2 = $48 million

Spain Co's shareholders have 75%, so France Co's shareholders have 25% (i.e. $12 million)

This is a gain of $2 million.

200 B

If GGG Co buys another company and values the target company on a higher P/E ratio, and if there is no synergy, there will be a reduction in the earnings per share of GGG Co (D). Since the acquisition is paid for by using new shares, the gearing ratio of GGG Co will fall (A), and existing shareholders will own a smaller proportionate stake in the company (C). It is unlikely that the share price will increase; in view of the reduction in earnings per share, it is more likely that the share price will fall after the takeover.

201 B, D

Stone Co has high gearing so increasing gearing further would be unwise ((A) and (E)).

Low cash reserves would rule out a cash offer funded from existing resources (C).

With a wide range of shareholders, a rights issue should be successful (D), or a share for share exchange could be used (B) because none of the existing shareholders seem to have control, so they would be less concerned about dilution issues.

202 A

Total value of the combined company will be:

(12m × $6.76) + (3m × $1.97) + 2m = $89.03m

The number of shares in the combined company will be:

12 m + [(1/3) × 3m] = 13m

Therefore the share price will be $89.03m/13m = $6.85

203 C

Bootstrapping can be used to find the post-acquisition value of combined companies assuming that the buying company's P/E ratio exceeds that of the seller.

The value is computed by applying Udika's P/E ratio to the combined current earnings of both entities.

204 A

205 A

Current values:

Oban 126m shares × $4.00 = $504m

Reeves 20m × $4.25 = $85m

Total is $589m

Oban's EPS = $25.2m/126m shares = $0.20

Oban's P/E ratio = $4.00/$0.20 = 20

Post-acquisition values

Oban's PAT = $25.2m

Reeves PAT = 20m shares × $0.34 = $6.8m

Combined PAT = $32m

Value using Oban's P/E = $32m × 20 = $640m

Synergy valued at $640 – $589 = $51m

206 C

(A), (B) and (D) certainly would be problems in this situation.

The fact that Fitness Co has very little cash (C) is irrelevant. In a share for share exchange no cash is paid.

207 A

Current wealth is $6.90 × 30 million = $207 million

After the takeover, total value of the combined entity will be

$207 million + $8 million + (5m × $12.84) = $279.2 million

There will be 40 million shares in issue (being 30 million existing shares and 10 million new shares issued in the share exchange with JJJ).

Hence, MMM's shareholders will own 30/40 = 75% of the combined entity, with a value of (75% × $279.2 million =) $209.4 million.

So the gain in wealth is $2.4 million ($209.4 million – $207 million).

208 The market believes that the shareholders of **YZ** will receive most of the benefit from this acquisition.

This could be because the value of the offer is too **high.**

209 Compared to a cash offer, a share for share exchange is **less** likely to create a liability to capital gains tax.

A share for share exchange will benefit the target company's shareholders more than a cash offer if the combined entity performs **well** after the acquisition.

210 C

An earnout would make some of the consideration dependent of future performance, so the directors of Z would be encouraged to continue working for the combined company and to improve its performance as much as possible.

211 D

Given the current share prices, it appears that the MQ shareholders would be indifferent if an offer of 2.23 LP shares to 1 MQ share were offered. However, they would be more likely to accept a bid that offered them a premium over the current value, so the best of the four choices – (D) in this case – is the MOST likely to be acceptable.

212 B

Current value of Astor Co = (23.5 × 9 =) $211.5 million

Current value of Baker Co = (9.5 × 7 =) $66.5 million

So the total value of the two companies is $278.0 million

Bootstrapping means applying the larger company's P/E ratio to the combined earnings, so post acquisition value = 9 × (23.5 + 9.5) = $297.0 million

i.e. a gain of $19.0 million

213 B

Value of Glenderaterra Co = $3.88 × 50m = $194.0 million

Value of Mungrisdale Co = $1.10 × 12m = $13.2 million

Therefore, value of the combined entity will be $194.0m + $13.2m + $10m = $217.2 million

Number of shares in the combined entity will be 50m + [(1/3) × 12m] = 54 million

Hence the share price post acquisition will be ($217.2m/54m) = $4.02

Mungrisdale Co shareholders will hold 4 million of the combined entity's shares, with a total value of $16.08 million. This is a gain of (16.08 – 13.2 =) $2.88 million.

i.e. approximately 29% of the total gain of $10 million

214 C

A debt for share exchange enables the target company shareholders to maintain an interest in the combined entity, but preserves the balance of control for the bidding company's shareholders (C).

If the target company shareholders want to realise cash for their investment (A) or if the bidding company is highly geared (B), a debt for share exchange would not be suitable.

(D) is irrelevant.

215 C

Current wealth is $6.90 × 30 million = $207 million

After the takeover, total value of the combined entity will be

$207 million + $8 million + (5m × $12.84) = $279.2 million

Since JJJ's shareholders' share of this value is the cash received of ($13.50 × 5 million =) $67.5 million, MMM's share will be (balancing figure) $211.7 million, which is $4.7 million more than it was before.

216 C

Current value of Big is 11m × $4 = $55 million

Current value of Small is 8m × $2.75 = $22 million

After the takeover, total value of the combined entity will be

$55 million + $22 million + $7.5m synergies = $84.5 million

After the acquisition, the total number of shares will be = 11m (owned by Big's existing shareholders) + 4m (now owned by Small's shareholders due to the 1 for 2 exchange) = 15m shares.

Therefore the new share price of Big will be $84.5m / 15m shares = $5.633

So the new wealth of the Small shareholders = 4m shares × $5.633 = 22.5m

Therefore, the wealth of Small's shareholders have increased from $22m to $22.5m – an increase of 2.3%. (Big's shareholders' wealth rose by 12.6%).

217 A

For Frodo:

Current value = 5m × $4.93 = $24.65m

P/E ratio = Price / Earnings = $24.65m / $1.45m = 17

For Sam:

Current value = 7m × $3.10 = $21.7m

P/E ratio = Price / Earnings = $21.7m / $1.55m = 14

When bootstrapping it is assumed that the combined entity will have the same P/E ratio as the buying company (Frodo).

Combined entity:

Earnings = $1.45m + $1.55m = $3m

P/E ratio (assumed to be the same as for Frodo due to bootstrapping) = 17

Value of the combined entity = P/E ratio ×Earnings = 17 × $3m = $51m

Synergies = Value of combined entity − total values of separate entities

= $51m − ($24.65m + $21.7m) = $4.7m

218 D

We need to first 'degear' the industry average beta, to find the asset beta, then 'regear' this asset beta to find a suitable equity beta that takes into account the gearing risk of the target company. **Note:** It is the target company's gearing which is relevant here, not Zeynab's gearing.

Degear the industry equity beta (using the formula in your formula sheet):

$\beta_u = \beta_g \times E/(E + D(1 - t))$

[**Note:** As debt is risk free, β_d is zero so the second part of the equation in the formula sheet can be ignored]

$\beta_u = 1.14 \times 75/(75 + 25(1 - 0.3))$

$\beta_u = 0.92$

Then use this, along with the target's gearing to find an appropriate βg

$\beta_u = \beta_g \times E/(E + D(1 - t))$

$0.92 = \beta_g \times 5/(5 + 2(1 - 0.3))$

$0.92 = \beta_g \times 0.781$

$\beta_g = 0.92 / 0.781 = 1.18$

219 A

A bank loan would be the best option since it would have no impact on control and raising gearing may actually benefit Maya and allow the company to benefit from additional tax relief.

An IPO would require the Maya family to lose control of the business, a bond issue is usually only available for a listed company and retained earnings may not be available and is likely to cause dividends to be cut.

220 C

CIV:

PBT = $2.77m

Expected profit based on tangible assets = 18% × $9m = $1.62m

Excess profit before tax due to intangible assets = $2.77m − $1.62m = $1.15m

Deduct off tax = $1.15m × 0.7 = $0.805m

Value of the intangibles = discount this as a perpetuity at the WACC = $0.805m / 0.15 = $5.4m

Therefore total value = $9m (tangible) + $5.4m (intangible) = $14.4m.